8 23

Global Communications in the Space Age

Toward a New ITU

Report of an International Conference sponsored
by the John and Mary R. Markle Foundation
and the Twentieth Century Fund

John and Mary R. Markle Foundation/New York
The Twentieth Century Fund/New York
1972

Previous publications on satellite communications

Communicating by Satellite
Report of the Twentieth Century Fund Task Force on International Satellite Communications
Background paper by Paul L. Laskin
The Twentieth Century Fund/1969

Communicating by Satellite: An International Discussion
Report of an International Conference sponsored by the Carnegie Endowment for International Peace and the Twentieth Century Fund
by Gordon L. Weil
Carnegie Endowment for International Peace and the Twentieth Century Fund/1969

The Future of Satellite Communications: Resource Management and the Needs of Nations
Second Report of the Twentieth Century Fund Task Force on International Satellite Communications
Appendices by Walter R. Hinchman and D. A. Dunn
The Twentieth Century Fund/ 1970

Planning for a Planet: An International Discussion on the Structure of Satellite Communications
Report of an International Conference sponsored by the Carnegie Endowment for International Peace and the Twentieth Century Fund
Carnegie Endowment for International Peace and the Twentieth Century Fund/1971

Library of Congress Catalog Card No. 72–83796/SBN
87078-128-6
Copyright © 1972 by The Twentieth Century Fund
Manufactured in the United States of America

The John and Mary R. Markle Foundation is concerned with improving the educational uses of the mass media and communications technology.

The Twentieth Century Fund, founded in 1919 and endowed by Edward A. Filene, devotes the major share of its resources to research, concentrating on objective and critical studies of institutions.

Foreword

International telecommunication has been extending its importance and influence with increasing rapidity in recent years. It is vital to the growth of world trade and it is the key medium for the dissemination of information on a global scale. Yet the users of international telecommunication in homes, offices, schoolrooms, public meeting places and private executive suites have had almost no involvement in the formulation of national or international policies dealing with telecommunication. This field, until now, has been left mostly to technical experts, whose achievements, it should be acknowledged, are considerable. But technological progress in telecommunication has now reached a state where international coordination and cooperation are essential. This stage calls for the participation of citizens everywhere in determining the priorities of communications technology so that the national governments responsible for international decisions can be made more aware of the need to transform this technology into a servant for all mankind.

Over the past several years, the Twentieth Century Fund has been seeking to broaden public awareness of the potential of satellite communications. In 1969 it established a Task Force on International Satellite Communications, the first independent group in the field, which issued an instructive report that drew attention to the desirability of international cooperation. A year later, the Task Force produced a second report that stressed the need for international coordination and planning. In addition, the Fund collaborated with the Carnegie Endowment for International Peace in sponsoring two international conferences on satellite communications. These conferences, which brought together authorities from many different countries, addressed the multiple problems raised by fast-advancing technology in the operation and regulation of communications by satellite. The reports of these conferences also were given wide dissemination in an effort to stimulate public understanding of and interest in telecommunications policy.

All of the previous task force and conference reports called for an international organization, preferably the International Telecommunication Union (ITU), to take an active role in guiding the development of international communications. ITU is the specialized agency of the United Nations involved in the regulation of international telecommunications. Because next year its member nations will meet to consider restructuring it, ITU was chosen as the focus of another international conference, jointly sponsored by the John and Mary R. Markle Foundation and the Fund, and held in Sidi Ferruch, Algeria.

The site of the conference itself is not without significance. Algeria is a developing country with all of the problems that confront other states that have gained their sovereignty in the age of telecommunication. Previous meetings had noted that the developing countries now make up a majority of the membership of ITU and will play a decisive role in its future. The choice of location for the conference not only signaled recognition of this role but also gave the participants a firsthand sense of the special importance of telecommunication to the entire developing world.

It is appropriate and timely to re-examine ITU. In an era when all institutions, national and international, are undergoing intensified scrutiny and criticism, ITU cannot—and should not—enjoy immunity. It has done useful work, but, like many other institutions, it was created before the globe had shrunk to its present compact size and before the advent of technological miracles that threaten to shrink it—and complicate it—still further.

But these changes are not necessarily a threat to ITU. They also represent challenge and opportunity. The conference in Algeria implicitly recognized ITU's potential as a forum within which nations can work together on telecommunications policy. Optimism characterized the quest for ways and means to reshape ITU so that it can be more responsive and adaptable to contemporary and future human needs.

Starting with the common assumption that communications technology is too important to be left solely to technicians, the conference explored and debated various means to broaden the scope of ITU so that in the future it can effectively address the cultural, economic and political aspects of telecommunication policy. The specific recommendations that emerged from the conference are designed to achieve this objective in a constructive and realistic fashion.

As an observer at Sidi Ferruch, I can attest to the international character of the meeting. Ably chaired by Jean d'Arcy, the conference's participants were given ample opportunity to air their individual views. The diversity of the participants guaranteed differences in opinion. But what proved most striking was the sustained effort of all the participants to reach agreement on the variety of issues discussed. While they did not reach a consensus on every subject, their demonstration of cooperation should serve as an example to the official delegations that will be meeting to consider the restructuring of ITU.

*   *   *

Both the John and Mary R. Markle Foundation and the Twentieth Century Fund wish to express their appreciation to the participants at the conference and to Jean d'Arcy, as its chairman. In addition to the report itself, the following pages contain background papers by Abram Chayes, Victor A. Haffner, Harold K. Jacobson, Edward Ploman and Jean Voge. These papers were specifically prepared for the conference and contain the individual views of their authors. We are grateful to them as well.

M. J. Rossant
Director
The Twentieth Century Fund

April 1972

Contents

Participants

Jean d'Arcy (Conference Chairman)
formerly *Direrctor,*
Radio and Visual Service Division
Office of Public Information
United Nations, New York, U.S.A.

Abd el Kader Bairi
Ministry of Post and
*   Telecommunications*
Algiers, Algeria

Lucius D. Battle
Vice President for Corporation
*   Relations*
Communications Satellite Corporation
Washington, D.C., U.S.A.

Abram Chayes
Professor of Law
Harvard Law School
Cambridge, Massachusetts, U.S.A.

Neville Clarke
Independent Television Authority
London, England

John Goormaghtigh
Director
European Center, Carnegie
*   Endowment for International Peace*
Geneva, Switzerland

Toki Hachifuji
The ITU Association of Japan, Inc.
Tokyo, Japan

Harold K. Jacobson
Center for Political Studies
Institute for Social Research
The University of Michigan
Ann Arbor, Michigan, U.S.A.

Carlos A. Killian
Empresa Nacional de
*   Telecomunicaciones*
Buenos Aires, Argentina

Leonard H. Marks
Lawyer
Washington, D.C., U.S.A.

Edward McWhinney
Director of International and
*   Comparative Legal Studies*
Indianapolis Law School
Indianapolis, Indiana, U.S.A.

Edward W. Ploman
Executive Director
International Broadcast Institute
London, England

Andres Rozental
Alternate Representative of Mexico
Mision Permanente de Mexico
Ante la Organizacion de los Estados
*   Americanos*
Washington, D.C., U.S.A.

Jerzy Rutkowski
Polish Academy of Sciences
Institute of Telecommunications
Warsaw, Poland

Krishan Sondhi
Indian Space Research Organization
Ahmedabad, India

Erik N. Valters (Rapporteur)
Chief, Central Programme Section
Radio and Visual Services Division
Office of Public Information
United Nations
New York, New York, U.S.A.

Erwin D. Canham (Observer)
Editor in Chief
The Christian Science Monitor
Boston, Massachusetts, U.S.A.

Georges-Henri Martin (Observer)
Editor-in-Chief
La Tribune de Genève
Geneva, Switzerland

Failure to assert the primacy of policy over technology is an alarming and increasingly dangerous phenomenon of the modern world. All too often, those responsible for the future development of technology are insufficiently aware of the far-reaching political, economic and social implications of their choices.
This danger is present also in the area of communication. Unless that danger is removed, future developments in the field of communication may well produce consequences which were neither foreseen nor desired from a more comprehensive national and international perspective. Often such consequences can only be modified later at considerable cost, if at all.

Kurt Waldheim
Secretary-General of the United Nations

28 March 1972

The Twentieth Century Fund

Post Office Box 184
West Haven, Connecticut 06516

We take pleasure in sending you GLOBAL COMMUNI-
CATIONS IN THE SPACE AGE: Toward a New ITU,
Report of an International Conference Sponsored by the
John and Mary R. Markle Foundation and the Twentieth
Century Fund. The report contains pioneering proposals
for safeguarding the future of international communications by strengthening the International
Telecommunication Union in coping with advancing
telecommunications technology and its impact on trade
and understanding among the peoples of the world. This
work is being sent without charge to a limited number of
officials and professionals in the communications field.

Requests for additional copies and bulk orders will be
fulfilled until the inventory is depleted.

Also available (free on request) **THE FUTURE OF
SATELLITE COMMUNICATIONS:** Resource Manage-
ment and the Needs of Nations, Second report of the
Twentieth Century Fund Task Force on International
Satellite Communications. With appendices on Issues in
Spectrum Resource Management by Walter R. Hinchman
and on A Possible World Communication Satellite System
Using 1970 Technology by D. A. Dunn.

REPORT OF THE CONFERENCE

Report of the Conference

Introduction

The speed of technological progress in the field of satellite communications confronts the international community with vast opportunities as well as complex problems. In March 1972, twenty experts from fourteen nations met in Algiers to discuss some of these problems and opportunities. The group, brought together by the John and Mary R. Markle Foundation and the Twentieth Century Fund, included communications engineers, lawyers, political economists, representatives of the telecommunications industry and officials of government and international organizations.

The objective of the Algiers Conference was to provide an independent and informal forum for exchanging information and views about international satellite communications in a framework designed to serve the public's need for knowledge of this vitally important subject. For, as most participants acknowledged, policy decisions affecting international telecommunications have lagged behind the pace of technological advance in telecommunications. Unless governments and their citizens have an awareness of the significance of the developments, present and potential, in international communications, there is a prospect that important policy decisions will be determined by technological convenience rather than the public good.

None of the participants spoke as a representative of his country or organization; each contributed his expert knowledge and expressed his opinions as an individual. For that reason the report on the conference that follows does not identify by name or affiliation the speakers whose remarks it summarizes.

Discussion at the conference focused on the International Telecommunication Union (ITU), a specialized agency of the United Nations concerned with the coordination and regulation of telecommunications among its 141 member countries, which will meet in Plenipotentiary Conference in September 1973. ITU is one of the oldest extant international organizations, dating back to the signing of the International Telegraph Convention in 1865. About once every decade since then, Plenipotentiary Conferences have met to renegotiate what is now called the International Telecommunication Convention, of which ITU is the creature. The Convention, and ITU as well, does not reflect a unified perspective on international communications. On the contrary, each successive Plenipotentiary Conference has added its particular concerns to those of its predecessors. But the last Plenipotentiary Conference, at Montreux in 1965, agreed that the next one, in 1973, should work toward the adoption of a permanent Charter or Constitution for ITU.

The 1973 ITU Plenipotentiary Conference thus posed a challenge to which the Algiers meeting was a deliberate response. The participants recognized the positive achievements of ITU. It has survived as a framework for international cooperation through 107 years and two World Wars. By allocating frequencies and promoting standardization of equipment and procedures, it has provided a foundation for the rapid expansion of international telecommunications over the last two decades. But the participants at the Algiers Conference agreed that ITU needs reform to meet the increasing demands arising from this very revolution in modern telecommunications.

The participants at the Algiers meeting saw some danger that the adoption of a Constitution might serve merely to perpetuate ITU's present structural inadequacies. But they also saw the forthcoming Plenipotentiary Conference as an opportunity for ITU to free itself of its complex and somewhat haphazard structure and to transform itself into a modern, unified institution equipped to meet the demands of the era of global telecommunication. This report, which summarizes the discussions in Algiers, recommends changes in ITU for this purpose.

A dominant theme of the conference was the importance of dealing with technical communications issues in the context of their economic, political and social ramifications. No one proposed that ITU be politicized; nor was there any suggestion that technical questions should be complicated by the introduction of irrelevant ideological considerations. But decisions in the field of international telecommunications affect the vital interests of every country in the world. Most participants believed that ITU delegations, lacking clear policy directives from their governments, are unable to formulate a coherent international communications policy as a basis for their technical decisions. As a result, they make technical decisions on an *ad hoc* basis that frequently proves harmful to the international community.

These decisions determine the conditions under which a country may establish or join a communications satellite system, international or domestic; the size and cost of earth stations for satellite transmission; the allocation and distribution of the limited international resources—the radio frequency spectrum and the geostationary orbit[1]—required for satellite communications; the promotion or inhibition of the development of particular modes or techniques of telecommunication; and the use of broadcast satellites for mass education and training in the developing

[1] "Radio transmission—the transfer of messages by electromagnetic radiation through space rather than along wires or cables—employs a limited natural resource, the radio frequency spectrum. The radio frequency spectrum is the range of frequencies (rates of oscillation) of electromagnetic radiation. Radio frequency serves to differentiate radio signals, just as the frequencies of sound waves permit them to be distinguished as different tones of the sound scale. Two radio transmission systems may not employ the same frequencies at the same time from the same place and over the same area without interfering with one another. Hence, wise use of the spectrum resource involves the careful coordination of several factors—frequency, location, direction of transmission, time of use—by which one radio transmission may be distinguished from another to avoid interference. . . .
"The geostationary orbit [is] the band of space in which satellites circle the earth at a speed equal to its rotation and appear to hang motionless above a fixed point on the earth's surface. This band lies 22,300 miles above the equator. The number of satellites which can be accommodated along this orbit is a major determinant of potential satellite communications capacity. The finite character of the geostationary orbit has led to the belief that 'orbital parking space' is a limited resource that must be carefully controlled and allocated."
(*The Future of Satellite Communications: Resource Management and the Needs of Nations*, Second Report of the Twentieth Century Fund Task Force on International Satellite Communications, The Twentieth Century Fund, New York, 1970, pp. 9–10).

5

countries. Unless the policy implications of these—and other—issues are addressed, the related technical decisions may have far-reaching, unanticipated and undesirable economic, political and social consequences.

Reform of ITU is not the only major problem facing international communications. The conference recognized, for example, that technical virtuosity alone cannot ensure that modern telecommunications will be employed to their fullest potential for education and for broadening and enriching international understanding. It also recognized a major problem confronting many countries planning satellite communications, namely, their ability to get their satellites launched without submitting to political or other discriminatory conditions. While participants agreed on the significance of this range of problems, the conference decided to confine its recommendations to reform of ITU because it believed that structural changes in the union are urgently needed and must be considered at the 1973 Plenipotentiary Conference.

In emphasizing reform of ITU, some participants at the conference were particularly concerned about the significance of international telecommunications for the developing countries. One of them declared that countries in the midst of a population explosion require direct broadcast satellites and programs of birth control information for mass audiences; he spoke of the sense of despair in the developing countries, the fear that those who were most in need of them would be cut off from the benefits of the new communications technology. His remarks served to highlight the underlying problem that confronted the Algiers Conference and would face the 1973 Plenipotentiary Conference: Can existing institutions be restructured efficiently enough and quickly enough to make technological capabilities meet human needs?

Functions of ITU

Briefly stated, the present ITU machinery consists of:

- A *Plenipotentiary Conference* composed of all member countries and meeting approximately every seven years to revise the International Telecommunication Convention.

- An *Administrative Council* composed of twenty-nine elected members, regionally balanced, meeting each year for ap-

6

proximately one month to direct ITU's affairs between Plenipotentiary Conferences;

- *Administrative Conferences* meeting at intervals of several years to revise the regulations allocating radio frequencies and establishing procedures for international communication by radio and, from time to time, for telephone and telegraph.

- Two technical *International Consultative Committees* (CCI's), one for radio (CCIR) and one for telephone and telegraph (CCITT), each comprised of plenary assemblies, periodically convened study groups, and full-time specialized secretariats; the committees make recommendations on technical specifications for equipment.

- An *International Frequency Registration Board* (IFRB), composed of five elected members, with its own specialized secretariat, that receives notification from countries seeking to use a particular radio frequency; the IFRB maintains a Master Register of frequencies, and if the proposed use conforms to the regulations, gives it a legitimate status by entering it on its Register.

- A *General Secretariat* with an elected Secretary General and an elected Deputy Secretary General; the Secretary General is charged with the administrative aspects of ITU's work but lacks authority to establish basic policy.

Changes in this organizational structure should reflect a coherent assessment of the functions ITU should be prepared to undertake in the future. The conference participants, although differing on details, were broadly agreed on the elements of these functional requirements. They are:

(1) Formulation of general policies and guidelines concerning major telecommunications issues, such as priorities among various communications services, between terrestrial radio communications and space systems, and between the goals of cost savings and frequency conservation;

(2) Allocation of the radio frequency spectrum;

(3) Medium and long-range planning to meet future international communications needs and to ensure optimum use of limited communications resources in terms of economic, technical

and equity considerations; in particular, a flexible planning mechanism for space communications;

(4) Collection, analysis and dissemination of information at the international level concerning not only each nation's present use of international facilities but also anticipated communications requirements and technical problems;

(5) Elaboration and enforcement of regulations and procedures, in accordance with established policies, for the conduct of international communications and domestic communications with international implications;

(6) Aid in the resolution of conflicts and disputes involving the application of such regulations and procedures;

(7) Development of equipment standards, operating procedures, training programs and other factors involved in improving telecommunications systems; the objectives should be not only technical innovation but also simplification and more reliable service.

(8) Technical assistance to developing countries in international communications and domestic uses of new technology, as well as help in formulating their positions on telecommunications matters of international concern.

The essential task of the 1973 Plenipotentiary Conference is to give ITU both the mandate and the power to perform these diverse and vital functions. The structural changes proposed by the Algiers Conference are designed to achieve these objectives.

Summary of Major Recommendations

(1) *Membership in the ITU should be open to all the countries of the world.*

(2) *A World Communications Assembly should be established as a major organ of ITU, providing a forum for the review of global policy issues at the highest level and at regular intervals.*

(3) *ITU should be given the capacity for flexible planning, including frequency allocation and regulation at the global level, particularly in connection with space communications. In addition, ITU's facilities for collection and analysis of statistical and other communications data should be greatly improved.*

(4) *ITU should expand and institutionalize its role in the adjustment of disputes among its members.*

(5) *An international communications research center should be established within ITU, to supplement work at present done at the national level and to provide disinterested advice, particularly to the developing countries.*

(6) *ITU should strengthen and expand its technical assistance activities.*

(7) *The ITU Secretariat should be reinforced and strengthened; its disparate elements should be unified and its capacities, particularly for communications planning, research and technical assistance, should be improved.*

Universality of ITU's Membership

Membership in ITU should be open to all the countries of the world. The participants noted that the effectiveness of ITU in dealing with the problems of international telecommunications depend on the extent to which nations participate in its work and adhere to its rules and regulations. Adherence to these rules and regulations is in the interest of all nations, and without universality of membership ITU cannot be fully effective in carrying out its global mandate. At present (as of April 1972) ITU's membership stands at 141. The major absentee, the People's Republic of China, has been admitted to the United Nations and is now eligible for ITU membership. East Germany, North Korea and North Vietnam are still excluded. Since international telecommunications is a concern of all nations, the conference expressed the conviction that the principle of universality of membership in ITU should be adopted and practiced.

Formulation of General Policies

A World Communications Assembly should be established as a major organization of ITU, providing a forum for the review of global policy issues at the highest level and at regular intervals.

The conference participants agreed that major policy issues implicit in ITU's regulatory function are not being addressed by governments at the international level in a timely or systematic fashion. Among these issues are general guidelines for the preservation and use of the limited international resources of the frequency spectrum and of the geostationary orbit, as well as priorities among various communications services, between terrestrial radio communications and space systems, and between considerations of cost and of frequency conservation. Still another issue, of major importance to developing countries, is the future of direct satellite broadcasting to community and home receivers. According to one member of the group in Algiers, the 1971 World Administrative Radio Conference for Space Telecommunications, which made technical decisions regarding direct broadcasting that were restrictive in effect, never considered the fundamental question of whether direct broadcasting ought to be promoted or restricted.

It is evident that unless ITU creates a high-level forum for the periodic and comprehensive review of policy issues, many important decisions affecting the future of international communications will continue to be made as though they were governed by technical considerations alone.

If the 1973 Plenipotentiary Conference results in the adoption of a permanent constitution for ITU, future conferences will be freed from the time-consuming task of renegotiating the numerous articles of the International Telecommunication Convention; they could then devote themselves to considering international communications policy issues. Accordingly, the Algiers group proposed that the permanent constitution for ITU transform the present Plenipotentiary Conference into a forum for high-level policy discussion. This transformation would be symbolized by changing its name to the World Communications Assembly.

To fulfill its functions, the World Communications Assembly should convene more frequently than the Plenipotentiary Conference—at intervals of not more than two or three years. It also should be empowered to hold special sessions when warranted by the needs of the international community.

In general, the participants agreed that the World Communications Assembly should not be dominated, as other ITU meetings now are, by telecommunications officials. As the highest legislative organ in the field of international telecommunications, the Assembly should be composed of broadly representative delegations appointed at the governmental level; these delegations must bring to bear on the ITU policy-making process not only technical but also economic, social and cultural considerations as well as value judgments among policy alternatives. This kind of representation obviously requires continuous and effective co-ordination on communications matters within national governments among the different departments affected. In the view of most participants, interested U.N. specialized agencies, international operating entities such as Intelsat, and users of international communications such as regional broadcasting unions also should be effectively represented in the proposed Assembly.

Despite this consensus, one of the participants in Algiers pointed out the danger of injecting the sort of factors into ITU that have contributed to the failure of other international agencies. Considerable care would be needed to ensure that the World Communications Assembly addressed itself to the most significant policy issues. Because the usual format of general assembly debate has not worked well in other organizations, the participants agreed that the ITU Secretariat and its council ought to have a role in formulating and presenting policy issues so that the Assembly could address them as they bear on ITU's practical work.

The participants considered that the World Communications Assembly's responsibilities should include:

(1) Over-all direction of ITU's technical work, particularly that of the Administrative Conferences and of the two International Consultative Committees.

(2) Establishment of broad outlines for planning.

(3) Elaboration of technical assistance policies.

(4) Election of ITU officials, which should be the Assembly's responsibility exclusively. (But the number of elected ITU officials should be reduced; only the Secretary-General and the members of the International Frequency Registration Board should be elected.)

(5) Convening of administrative conferences and determining their agenda and terms of reference.

(6) Over-all control of the ITU's budget with regard to both expenses and ways and means.

(7) Adoption of amendments to the new ITU constitution, subject to ratification by the membership.

The Assembly cannot perform these functions effectively or efficiently without adequate budgetary power. In the view of the participants, if the constitution establishes a fixed system of budgetary assessment, the Assembly should administer it. The Assembly should also explore potential new sources of revenue for the ITU. In the past, as more than one participant noted, a major constraint on ITU's activities has been that its budget is financed by national telecommunications administrations, which are expected to break even if not to show a profit.

The participants felt that in the intervals between meetings of the Assembly, and within limits set by the Assembly, the work of the organization should be conducted by the ITU Administrative Council, to be renamed the Communications Council. The Council would receive directives from the Assembly and help to frame policy issues for submission to the Assembly. The Council could be maintained at its present size of twenty-nine members and should retain adequate regional representation.

Planning and Management

ITU should be given the capacity for flexible planning, including frequency allocation and regulation at the global level, particularly in connection with space communications. In addition, ITU's facilities for collection and analysis of statistical and other communications data should be greatly improved.

Traditionally, ITU's main task has been the elaboration of accepted regulations and procedures for the conduct of international communications as well as of domestic communications with international implications. This work will continue to be essential, and the traditional machinery of specialized ITU conferences still seems the most suitable framework for it. But an effective World Communications Assembly, the participants felt, could facilitate the efforts of the conferences by providing them with the broad policy guidelines they require to respond effectively to the needs of the international community.

But ITU's effectiveness as the manager of the world's finite communications resources will depend primarily on the strengthening of its planning function, particularly with regard to space communications.

For the past decale, ITU has maintained continual Regional Plan Commissions—for Europe, Africa, the Americas and Asia—and a World Plan Commission. These commissions are primarily engaged in traffic and circuit planning. They meet every four years and establish, on the basis of national requirement projections, both a "fixed plan" for the following four years and an approximate "informative plan" for the four years thereafter. The World Plan Commission, also meeting every four years, attempts to coordinate the regional plans.

The group in Algiers observed that a four-year interval may be too long to permit countries to respond adequately to the rapid changes in their traffic demands and social needs. One participant described ITU's traffic and circuit-planning mechanism as suitable for terrestrial communications in homogeneous developed regions such as Europe but inappropriate and inadequate for the developing countries and for space communications.

Although traffic and circuit planning is reasonably effective, the participants felt that ITU's system governing the use of the radio frequency spectrum leaves much to be desired. At present the first step is the allocation of blocs of frequencies for specified uses or "services," such as marine navigation, radio astronomy, standard broadcasting. This task is performed by Administrative Radio Conferences made up of all ITU members and meeting at irregular and rather infrequent intervals. After the initial allocation, if a station in a particular country wants to use a frequency, the telecommunications administration of that country notifies the IFRB. In the event that the proposed use may cause harmful interference with an existing station, the country involved may object, and the two administrations may seek to adjust the matter bilaterally. But if the issue cannot be resolved, the proposed use will not be entered in the Master Register. In effect, therefore, within the blocs of frequencies allocated by the Administrative conferences, the board operates on a principle of "first come, first served."

The 1971 World Administrative Radio Conference on Space Telecommunications passed a general resolution that qualified the "first come, first served" principle. It also ruled that in some situations an existing satellite might be under some obligation to seek to accommodate or even to make way for a newer satellite system. These actions, although tentative, mark an important breakthrough in the direction of flexible planning for space systems. Even more important, the conference resolved that future conferences should be convened specifically to adopt world or regional plans for direct broadcasting from satellites. Unfortunately, the resolution did not set forth principles or procedures to guide such planning.

Many of the participants at Algiers were concerned that these new planning conferences, following ITU's traditional approach, would establish some kind of fixed division of the spectrum and orbit for satellite broadcasting in order to provide all countries with some minimal access to these resources. Such rigidity would be incapable of responding to new developments in a fast changing technology. Moreover, it might keep much of the orbit and spectrum unused in anticipation of future demands that might or might not materialize.

The alternative preferred by most of the participants was a flexible planning system. Flexibility, as they conceived it, would permit the fullest current use of the satellite broadcast medium while preserving the possibility of adjustment and rearrangement to meet the needs of latecomers.

Even though flexible planning was endorsed, the participants acknowledged that it raised a major problem—the investment resources already committed on the basis of previous plans. One of the participants, for instance, pointed out that television had been standardized in both the United States and Europe before the development of techniques that permit television to operate on much narrower frequency bands. Today, millions of television receivers are in use; they would have to be adapted or discarded to take advantage of this technological progress (this problem will be the subject of the 1974 World Administrative Radio Conference in Geneva).

By contrast, another participant observed that flexibility is both necessary and feasible for satellite communications because communications satellites have a relatively short life expectancy. Flexibility, he noted, should be built into transmitters and receivers in the first place. In fact, once the concept of flexible planning is firmly established, built-in flexibility of equipment will probably follow as a matter of course.

If ITU is to perform a planning function, the participants agreed that it must have adequate data and statistical material. Yet ITU today does not even publish a statistical yearbook. A participant commented that internationl data collection is hampered by the lack of national planning; even a highly developed country such as the United States has no over-all national projection of its future communications requirements. The developing countries are even less able to anticipate their needs. Communications satellite traffic between Argentina and Brazil doubled in the first year after earth stations were installed in each country and doubled again the next year. Other participants observed that experts in the field of frequency management are extremely scarce; for the most part they are needed for work in their own countries. But the Algiers group agreed on the need for a planning body that would serve the aggregate needs of the whole world.

The purpose of this global planning body would not be to belittle or to impair the role of national administrations in international telecommunications planning. Planning must be based on national requirements and is impossible without the cooperation of national administrations. So the objective of an institutionalized planning function in ITU could be to make possible a more comprehensive multilateral planning effort in the future, and to provide reliable guidelines for national administrations.

To carry out this planning function the ITU Secretariat requires a new specialized planning unit. The proposed unit would also collect, analyze and disseminate information and statistical data at the international level concerning not only the existing use of international facilities but also future needs.

Resolution of Conflicts and Disputes

ITU should expand and institutionalize its role in the adjustment of disputes among its members.

The products of ITU conferences, following their ratification by governments, represent instruments of international law that impose legal obligations on national telecommunications administrations. It is in the common interest of the international community that all national administrations strictly implement these obligations. However, ITU lacks both independent fact-finding authority and direct power to enforce its regulations. The law, as one participant commented, in international communications as in other areas, lags behind technology.

But while some means of imposing sanctions for violations of obligations may be desirable, there is an even greater need for a means of resolving conflicts and disputes involving the application of regulations and procedures. Traditionally, ITU members have preferred to settle their disputes through bilateral negotiations. One participant suggested the establishment of full-fledged judicial machinery, such as an Arbitral Tribunal or a World Communications Court, in a strengthened ITU. Most participants, though, felt that few cases were likely to be submitted for binding ruling by third-party judges. It was noted that ITU members have not used the compulsory arbitration procedure provided for in the International Telecommunication Convention; as in other fields, countries simply have not been willing to resort to arbitral tribunals with enforcement powers, nor are they likely to do so in the immediate future. Moreover, the controversies that can be foreseen will probably respond better to conciliation and adjustment than to judicial settlement.

The fact is that ITU already possesses an organ with the potential to exercise such a conflict-resolution function—the International Frequency Registration Board (IFRB). In its frequency registration work, the board is engaged in something comparable to the conciliation process for adjustment or disputes. The IFRB does not need new powers as such (although some formal recognition of its suggested conciliation function would be desirable), but rather a role in the coordination process at a sufficiently early stage, before positions harden.

The 1971 World Administrative Radio Conference served to strengthen the role of the IFRB in satellite communications by establishing a new coordination procedure. A national administration proposing to deploy a satellite network or system must notify the IFRB five years in advance. The board publishes the technical details of the proposed system and all administrations whose interests are affected, whether or not they already operate a satellite system, have the right to be heard in the coordination process. Any administration can request the assistance of the IFRB to help resolve conflicts. Before it can approve the use of the frequencies the IFRB must be satisfied that this coordination process has been carried out.

Given this background, the Algiers group recommended that an institutionalized conflict-resolution function should be established within ITU, with particular reference to the IFRB. The IFRB will be able to fulfill this additional function without any increase in its staff and resources if, as suggested below, a reinforced and strengthened ITU Secretariat takes over the present technical functions of the IFRB.

Communications Research

An international communications research center should be established within ITU to supplement work at present done at the national level and to provide disinterested advice, particularly to the developing countries.

Technical and operating questions regarding telecommunications are now dealt with by the International Radio Consultative Committee (CCIR) and the International Telegraph and Telephone Consultative Committee (CCITT) respectively. Each of these two consultative committees has a Plenary Assembly and a specialized secretariat of its own. Each also has numerous separate commissions and working groups.

This division encourages conflicts in authority, tends to produce inefficiency and waste of resources, and leads to duplication of work. A participant noted that the technical secretariats are staffed by fewer than thirty people, barely enough to handle the organizational paperwork.

Most important, the present arrangements make it difficult for most ITU members, particularly the developing countries, to make an effective contribution to the work of the CCIs. These difficulties are primarily attributable to the shortage of trained technicians in the developing countries. Moreover, since the actual work of the CCIs is done in a large number of subsidiary bodies, developing countries, with limited staffs at their disposal, cannot afford adequate coverage.

Because skilled technicians are scarce, it is not surprising that about 90 percent of the technical papers submitted to the CCIs by national administrations come from the six or seven countries with the greatest volume of international communications. Some of the parameters involved in CCI decisions therefore tend to be determined by the preoccupations of these countries. An example is the tendency of the CCIs to set very high equipment standards. One member of the group observed that the developing countries do not benefit from this concern for technical sophistication; he felt that their greatest need is for simplicity and low costs. But another participant responded that the cheapest equipment is not always the best for the developing countries; the equipment should be reliable and not require servicing. "We are too poor," he said, "not to buy good quality."

Still another participant felt that the fundamental problem, as international telecommunications are organized today, was that there is really no continuous arrangement under which a country can receive disinterested advice as to which system and what technology are most appropriate for its needs. Within the governments of individual countries, moreover, it is almost impossible to arrive at an interdisciplinary approach to communications problems. Another member of the group remarked that, because the big countries can ascertain their interests and fight for them, an independent source of expertise is needed as a countervailing power within ITU.

As a result of these views, the Algiers conference recommended the creation of an international center within the ITU framework—preferably as an integral part of the Secretariat—to supplement the communications research at present done at national levels. The research performed at this new center should be policy oriented; it should include the evaluation of economic and other implications of technical parameters and the determination of priorities for research at the national level. The new institution would be able to offer disinterested counsel on technical and related matters to developing countries. Such an institution might be called the Communications Research Center.

The group suggested that ITU convene a special international meeting to consider this subject. The major difficulty to be resolved would be the problem of generating adequate funds for the center. Various sources of financing should be explored, including governments, private foundations, and scientific or industrial organizations. The latter already share in defraying the expenses of the CCIs in whose work they participate, but their contributions should be made mandatory and firmly scaled rather than voluntary.

Technical Assistance

ITU should strengthen and expand its technical assistance activities.

There was general agreement at the Algiers Conference that the developing countries urgently need technical assistance—in the sense of pre-investment assistance—regarding international telecommunications systems and the use of new technology to meet their domestic needs. The conference recommended that such a function be entrusted to a revitalized ITU Secretariat.

The conditions that keep the volume of technical assistance low have both national and international roots. At the national level, development planners all too often have failed to understand the significance of communications in the over-all development process. At the international level, ITU's share of UNDP's operational funds was established years ago (ITU's current budget for technical assistance is less than $10 million a year, all of which comes from the United Nations Development Program (UNDP) for whose projects ITU acts as executing agency); attempts to increase it would meet with strong opposition from other UN specialized agencies.

Obviously, a substantial increase in the level of ITU technical assistance will require a new source of revenue. The participants agreed that although it might be undesirable to move away from the concept that development assistance funds should be centralized in the UNDP, the fact remains that a number of UN specialized agencies, including the Food and Agriculture Organization (FAO) and the World Health Organization (WHO), already finance some of their technical assistance from non-UNDP sources. One member of the group, noting that national administrations, because of their commercial character, were unlikely to be willing to make additional contributions to the ITU budget for the purpose of technical assistance, suggested that such contributions would probably have to come from the governments of ITU members.

The ITU Secretariat

The ITU Secretariat should be reinforced and strengthened; its disparate elements should be unified and its capacities, partic-

ularly for communications planning, research and technical assistance, should be improved.

The most striking feature of the present ITU structure, and the manner in which it differs most sharply from the other UN specialized agencies, is the division of the ITU staff into four autonomous units: the General Secretariat, the staff of the IFRB, and the specialized secretariats of the CCIR and the CCITT. The elected officials of these organs are responsible to different plenary groups. The Secretary-General, elected by the Plenipotentiary Conference and heading the General Secretariat, has only limited administrative powers over the other three organs and virtually no power over their substantive activities. (The Deputy Secretary-General is also elected by the Plenipotentiary Conference.) The work of the IFRB is determined by Administrative Radio Conferences which also elect the board's members. The work of the CCIR and CCITT secretariats and study groups is set by their Plenary Assemblies, composed of technical representatives of the ITU member countries, which also elect the directors of the two secretariats.

This cumbersome structure is a direct result of the history and development of the different ITU organs. The work of the ITU staff is so fragmented that, as one member of the group commented, the different organs, although housed in the same building, use different street addresses.

The conference believed that there is a clear case for combining the disparate elements of the ITU staff into a single ITU Secretariat headed by the Secretary-General. Such an arrangement would parallel that of the United Nations, in which appropriate staffs are permanently assigned to various UN organs but form parts of a single Secretariat.

The Secretary-General should be elected by the World Communications Assembly and should ultimately be responsible to the Assembly rather than to the Council, although he should work closely with the Council and have a seat at the Council table.

The Secretary-General should be considered an international executive and given scope for initiative. For example, he should be able to make substantive proposals of his own on matters of concern to ITU.

The suggested transformation of the Secretariat's role from routine tasks and administration into something with greater substantive involvement in the work of ITU has a number of important consequences for the Secretariat staff.

The participants saw the need for this unified and strengthened ITU Secretariat to help carry out the various suggestions made earlier in this report. In particular, they felt that the Secretariat should have new responsibilities in the fields of planning, research and technical assistance. The Secretariat should also be entrusted, to a larger degree than in the past, with the substantive preparation of ITU conferences. Until now, preparatory work has been the responsibility of the national delegations, and in the nature of things only a few of these could participate fully. In the future, the Secretariat might even organize a set of seminars or preparatory meetings prior to conferences, particularly for the benefit of the developing countries.

The participants agreed that the professional caliber of the staff must be improved through a whole new approach to recruitment and training. One group member suggested that the organization make greater use of national experts of high competence, seconded on a temporary basis. Conceivably, the double-contract system in use at CERN might be applied in ITU, with each career staff member receiving a long-term employment contract and a renewable fixed-term function contract. The geographical composition of the ITU Secretariat must move away from its present emphasis on staff members from Western Europe and particularly from Switzerland. Finally, the number of professional disciplines represented in the ITU Secretariat must be enlarged and should encompass not only administrators and engineers, but also economists, lawyers, development planners, social scientists, and the like.

Conclusion

The recommendations in this report build on the hundred years that ITU has been engaged in the increasingly complex task of coordinating and rationalizing international telecommunications. In this sense the past is prologue. But the participants in Algiers saw the 1973 Plenipotentiary Conference as an unparalleled opportunity to strengthen ITU so that it can meet the new and pressing demands imposed by both modern technology and widespread need. If ITU is to be a flexible and effective force, responsive and responsible, in international telecommunications, it must possess a coherent structure, a cohesive and efficient staff and clearer lines of authority.

Behind these seemingly dry and mundane organizational proposals lie a number of more general and more resonant themes. The participants in Algiers were agreed that international communications in the last third of the twentieth century are becoming truly global in scope. It is no longer simply a matter of working things out between close neighbors or among a few states sharing similar needs and perspectives. The international community has an obligation to assure all countries and peoples a voice in the shaping of international communications. This global objective cannot be accomplished by pursuing the traditional tinkering with the ITU mechanism. On the contrary it requires a reform of ITU and a determination to implement reform.

The newly available means of communication have special significance for the developing countries in their struggles for economic and social betterment. In this area, too, the international community has a special obligation to ensure that international telecommunications are employed most effectively.

In their deliberations, the participants recognized that it is no longer possible to ignore the economic and social consequences of technical decisions in the field of international telecommunications. The international community has the responsibility to address these policy issues systematically and explicitly, instead of permitting them to be resolved as by-products of technological decisions.

ITU is the instrumentality available for these international responsibilities. Decisive action is needed to give it the power to carry them out.

APPENDICES

APPENDIX A
Reforming ITU?
Abram Chayes

The International Telecommunication Union has not been the target of much praise in recent years. Yet it has resisted with surprising hardihood the ministrations of those, the present author included, who have come to bury it.

It is easy to inveigh against myopia and wrongheadedness in national and international telecommunications bureaucracies. More relevant would be an effort to account for ITU's unexpected structural durability. The organization must be doing something right. Identifying the activities that ITU has performed well should provide some guidance in formulating both the substantive goals and the political strategy of reform.

Over the years, ITU's principal function has been to provide a forum and procedures for the coordination of policy among national telecommunications administrations, particularly those of the eight or ten major communications powers. So long as international telecommunications problems were centered mainly in Europe the system worked well enough. If the major communicators could come to agreement on standards or equipment specifications, the lesser powers could adapt without too much difficulty, especially in international telegraph and telephone communications, which are impossible without some kind of coordination. In the field of standard band and short wave broadcasting, where coordination is not absolutely necessary and where there are payoffs for sheer power, ITU's efforts have been less successful.

ITU's institutional structure consists of a congeries of negotiating committees, much of whose work is done by subgroups. The proliferation of meetings is such that only the most important nations in the communications field can prepare for and cover any significant part of them. Participation in many of these groups is open to concerned private enterprises; hence the communications industry can sometimes use the meetings to work out its own coordination problems.

Ranged against these powerful governmental and industrial communications powers, the resources of ITU as an institution are limited. Its staff is weak and fragmented. ITU has almost no independent decision-making power; for the most part the output of its committees and conferences must be referred back formally to governments for ratification. And it has negligible authority to enforce regulations even when they are ratified, as they usually are. As at the time of enactment, bilateral negotiation and adjustment are the principal methods for assuring compliance and the role of the organization as such, even by way of mediation or good offices, is strictly limited.

As a forum for coordination of national policies, ITU has a long history stretching back to the Paris Conference of 1865. Not the least of the organization's assets is a tradition of cooperation between countries of Eastern and Western Europe that long antedates the Cold War. As a result, ITU has survived the wildly fluctuating political climate of the last two decades rather better than most other international organizations.

Assuming the foregoing picture is roughly accurate, what is wrong with it? Is there anything in it that demands reform other than on the grounds of organizational tidiness or from one-worlders seeking to extend the range of supranational authority? We may identify two principal ways in which the organizational concept described above is inadequate to today's requirements in the field of international telecommunications policy.

First, it does not provide sufficient representation for the interests and needs of the developing countries.

Second, it is not well adapted to problems calling for allocation or management of common resources, as opposed to coordination of national policies. Increasingly, international telecommunications problems are of the resource-management type.

Each of these points warrants some expansion.

The overwhelming majority of ITU's members are developing countries, and their numbers have increased over the past decade. These countries have disproportionately small representation in the governing bodies, among the officials and on the staff of the organization, and little influence upon its regulatory activities. Although the developing countries are not entitled to weight in the organization proportional to their numbers, they are surely entitled to more of a voice than they have at present.

ITU has responded to the needs of the developing countries mainly through efforts to provide technical assistance in the design and operation of communications systems. In this activity, ITU acts as the agent of the United Nations Development Program and technical assistance functions are financed outside the organization's regular budget. The amounts involved are not substantial, and in general this technical assistance function is seen as incidental to ITU's main work. Moreover, it is not clear that the staff is adequate to advise and assist the developing countries in terms that are relevant to their capabilities and situations. There is now a movement among the developing countries for an internally financed technical assistance program. It is not clear that this proposal can be approved in the near future, given the ITU budgetary system, or that, if implemented, it would improve the deficiencies in the present system.

On the regulatory side, ITU's structure militates against effective formulation of the special interests of developing countries and the elaboration of policies to vindicate those interests. Since the work of the organization takes place in a large number of negotiating conferences among national and industrial representatives, the key to influencing outcomes is the technical qualifications and thoroughness of preparation of these representatives. Technically trained personnel remain in very short supply in the developing areas, and the developing countries are simply not able to deploy delegations large enough or well enough prepared to protect their own interests.

Somewhat similar conditions prevailed for smaller European nations in the prewar period, but the consequences were not so serious. The interests of these countries did not diverge so sharply from those of the communications giants. They were at roughly the same technological stage. Economic imperatives for indigenous manufacture were not so strong. The regional environment in which they would operate was in any case dominated by their larger neighbors, and there was little opportunity for separate regional solutions. These factors operated to keep the solutions reached by ITU's coordinating mechanism relatively compatible with the interests of the smaller powers. None of these factors operates today to safeguard the interest of the developing countries.

Like the organization's membership, the problems on its agenda have changed radically in recent years. A gross index of these changes is the shift of the main business of the organization from telephone and telegraph to radiocommunications, a movement that has accelerated with the advent of satellite communications. For the telephone and telegraph, the principal questions are related to interconnection. These are well suited to the process of coordination of national policies. Moreover, there is a built-in sanction: to refuse to "coordinate" is to lose the power to communicate with the other party.

Similar questions also arise in radiocommunications, but they are not the only significant issues in the regulatory process. Moreover, the state that refuses to "coordinate" may still reach receivers in its neighbors' territory if it is willing to build a powerful enough transmitter. It is not strictly true, as is so often maintained, that nations must mutually respect some schedule of agreed frequency assignments on pain of creating a chaos in which none can be heard. That rule may hold for the small and the weak, but not, or at least not to the same degree, for a country that is willing to invest resources in preempting and maintaining control of a frequency.

This alteration in the reciprocity of available sanctions is only one of the changes wrought by radiocommunications in the character of the international regulatory problem. The most important change is the focus on regulation of the electromagnetic frequency spectrum, the vehicle for all radio communications. At first this problem was viewed as one of *allocation* of the spectrum among various uses and users. Latterly, it is seen more as a problem of *management* of the spectrum in order to optimize the use of a scarce resource. In either version, the requirements of the process go well beyond the coordination of national policies.

ITU's failure to achieve an orderly allocation of the spectrum for short wave and standard band broadcasting has already been mentioned. Even in situations where breakdown was not so conspicuous, the results have been far from ideal. For example, the European television plan promulgated by ITU in 1954, which is pointed to as a major accomplishment, is rigid and inflexible, probably unduly so. The Television Allocation Plan, announced by the Federal Communications Commission in 1952, to govern allocation of TV channels in the United States, shows these same characteristics, perhaps to a greater extent.

Since the FCC is structurally very different from ITU, the similarity of result suggests that something other than institutional malfunctions may be at work. It is argued that the requirement of a secure investment base, both for broadcasting and for the manufacture of receiving equipment, required the imposition of a fixed matrix on the industry. No doubt this need for stability of expectations had its impact. But it also seems to the author that this kind of rigid scheme is the type of "plan" that is most likely to emerge from a multilateral coordinating process. Moreover, the institutional differences between ITU and the FCC may be smaller than they seem, particularly in this kind of allocative rule making, where the commission may act more as a broker among competing interests than as an agency with independent policy making and enforcement authority.

The two deficiencies discussed above reinforce each other to some extent. And this approach in turn enhances the position of the technologically advanced countries. The increasing importance of space communication intensifies these problems. Communications satellites utilize a new and limited resource—the geostationary orbit. And because satellite technology particularly lends itself to the communications needs of the developing countries, it is a matter of urgency that the regulatory process should recognize their interests.

Proposals to change ITU must not only address its deficiencies but also take account of the formidable capacity for resisting reform that the organization has already demonstrated.

The first and most important need, in the author's opinion, is to unify and strengthen the technical staff of the organization. A strong, high quality staff will permit the organization to develop policy initiatives and positions independent, to some extent, of those of the strongest members. It can provide a spokesman for developing countries without technical resources of their own. And it will enable the organization to influence spectrum management in the general interest.

To this end, the separate staffs of the CCIR, the CCITT and IFRB should be consolidated with the General Secretariat. The unified secretariat should be subordinate to and under the direction of the Secretary-General. The quality of the staff should be improved by the use, for example, of the devices that have proved successful in assembling a first rate technical staff at the International Atomic Energy Agency: short terms of employment, secondment from governments and industry, greater use of consultants. Without sacrifice of quality, the staff should be diversified so as to reduce the present overwhelming dominance of Western Europeans.

The second major change would be an effort to institutionalize the planning function, particularly in the field of space communications. The recently concluded World Administrative Radio Conference has broadened and deepened the requirements for coordination of administrations contemplating space systems and has sought to dilute the priority of systems in place over newcomers. Yet in the end what is contemplated is a series of bilateral coordinations between the administration that is establishing a system and those that are affected by it, rather than a comprehensive spectrum management process. There is a call for world or regional planning conferences, but these seem designed to follow the format that led to the European television plan.

The Twentieth Century Fund Task Force in its second report proposes a space communication planning group of experts appointed by the Secretary-General and reporting to the political organs of ITU.[1] This still seems to the author to be the best approach. In view of the failure of the WARC to move in the direction of planning and the postponement of the Plenipotentiary Conference until 1973, the pressures may grow to a point where this concept could generate the necessary support.

If not, ITU should, at the very least, be brought into the coordinating procedures at an earlier stage and in a more forceful manner. The vehicle for this intervention should be the International Frequency Registration Board. Under the present procedure, in the early stages of coordination the board can function only as a messenger, and a party may use its good offices only after the bilateral coordinating process has come to a dead end. The board could be much more effective if it were at the table from the outset as counsel for the situation. Indeed, coordination should take place under IFRB auspices.

The board should be given similar mediating and good offices functions in connection with settlement of disputes among members, as the Twentieth Century Fund report recommends. The board would be freed for these more substantive functions if its ministerial, record-keeping and notification duties were transferred to the new, consolidated staff. The unified staff would provide technical backing for any new functions assigned to the board as well as its existing regulatory activities in the field of frequency registration.

Third, if the staff is consolidated it might not be inappropriate to continue the separate existence of the CCIR and CCITT under elected chairmen. These committees have developed important traditions of work and personal and professional connections that may be worth preserving, given the safeguard of a unified Secretariat. The remaining recommendations of the Twentieth Century Fund Task Force seem well worth pursuing. They involve, primarily, the shift to a charter form of governance. It would include:

(1) A continuing charter as the basic constitutive document of the organization. The charter would not have to be readopted at each session of the plenipotentiary organ.

[1]*The Future of Satellite Communications: Resource Management and the Needs of Nations,* second Report of the Twentieth Century Fund Task Force on International Satellite Communications, The Twentieth Century Fund, New York, 1970, p. 25.

(2) A plenary body of the membership, meeting once every two or four years on a schedule prescribed in the charter. All members of the organization would be represented in this body, which would set basic policy for the organization.

(3) A smaller representative council that would meet annually, or perhaps twice a year, between sessions of the plenary body. It would supervise the execution of policies promulgated by the plenary body and would have the power to adopt, at least for reference to governments, recommendations for changes in the regulations proposed by the CCIR and CCITT.

These changes should result in a more coherent and effective organization.

Fourth, ITU should become truly universal in membership. Current political developments augur well for this objective.

One may ask how, if the status quo is satisfactory, indeed preferable, to the dominant powers in the organization, these changes can possibly be implemented. Although this is not a political paper, it may be appropriate to note that the key to the situation is in the developing countries and their overwhelming numerical majority in the organization.

The developing countries will have an opportunity to use this numerical leverage at the 1973 Plenipotentiary Conference. It is important that these countries carefully articulate their strategy and goals before that conference. Public discussion of the kind we are engaged in can facilitate this process.

In 1973 the developing countries are likely to renew their demands for some form of internally financed assistance program. That is understandable. But they will forego a rare opportunity if they pursue this goal at the expense of reform in ITU's regulatory and organizational aspects.

APPENDIX B
Radio Frequency Spectrum Planning
Victor A. Haffner

Over the years one of the major problems of the International Telecommunication Union has been the allocation, assignment, registration and orderly use of radio frequencies.

ITU first confronted these problems at the Berlin Radiotelegraph Conference in 1906, which allocated frequencies of 500 KHz to 1000 KHz for public correspondence in the Maritime Mobile Service and frequencies below 380 KHz for long distance communications with coast stations.

In subsequent years, research made more of the frequency spectrum available for radio communication. In 1927, ITU allocated frequencies up to 30 MHz, in 1932 up to 60 MHz, in 1938 to 200 MHz, and, at the Atlantic City Conference in 1947, to 10.5 GHz. The Geneva Administrative Radio Conference in 1959 made allocations up to 40 GHz. (The lower limit remained at 10 KHz.)

At the time of the Atlantic City Radio Conference in 1947, some member nations attempted to record frequency uses in an orderly manner at the Berne bureau of the union. The Atlantic City Radio Conference, realizing how difficult managing the radio frequency spectrum would be, set up the International Frequency Registration Board. Article 12 of the International Telecommunication Convention set forth special regulations regarding the Board and Article 13 of the International Telecommunication Convention, Montreux 1965, defined its essential duties. It stipulated that the members of the board should serve not as representatives of their countries or of a region but as custodians of the international public trust.

In accordance with the International Telecommunication Convention, the IFRB has sought to effect an orderly recording of the frequency assignments of different member countries and to ensure the orderly use of frequencies in accordance with the radio regulations and any decisions taken by the conferences of the union. The IFRB also promotes international recognition of the technical criteria for shared frequency assignments, and it advises members of the union regarding the operation of services on those parts of the spectrum where harmful interference may occur.

In addition, the IFRB assists the developing countries in the selection of frequencies for their services that will not result in mutual interference with other services. The board also arranges for representatives of developing countries to visit its Secretariat at the ITU headquarters for training; it also arranges special seminars for developing countries, to train their representatives in the management of the radio frequency spectrum.

Although research in radio techniques is continuing in the developing countries, the developed countries possess a great deal of information on the economic use of the radio frequency spectrum and have contributed this information through their various representatives at international conferences to the IFRB.

But at the 1965 Montreux Plenipotentiary Conference certain proposals were submitted regarding the continued existence of the IFRB. Some developed countries did not see any further useful purpose for the IFRB as a specialized secretariat of the union. Only pressure from the developing countries preserved the IFRB in that capacity.

Today, only seven years later, political changes and technological progress, particularly in satellite communications and aeronautical and maritime fixed and mobile communications techniques, have more or less stretched to the limit the resources and capability of the IFRB.

ITU's member countries are normally guided in their use of the frequency spectrum by the Radio Regulations and the appendices attached thereto, which show the frequency bands allocated for the various radio services at past ITU Administrative Radio Conferences.

This arrangement places the developing countries at something of a disadvantage. At the time when the older member countries of the International Telecommunication Union agreed on the use and recording of frequencies for various radio services, a large number of developing countries were still in the colonial era. On their emergence to self-determination, they attempted to meet the frequency requirements for their various radio services and found that the older members of the union had already been assigned a greater part of the radio frequency spectrum for their own services.

Because suitable frequencies are not available for the broadcasting services of some developing countries, these countries have had to use instead certain frequencies which the Radio Regulations recommend for fixed services.

Although one of the IFRB's main duties at the Administrative Radio Conferences and Regional Conferences is to see that agreement is reached and recommendations made on the use of the radio frequency spectrum for various services, the problem of satisfying all users remains unresolved and will continue to do so for a very long time.

The advent of satellite communications, particularly the use of satellites in geostationary orbit, has complicated matters; frequencies in the VHF, UHF, and SHF bands are now being used for these services. To meet the world's communications needs, satellite and terrestrial systems must share frequencies. The problems of frequency sharing lend additional urgency to the need for a very powerful international institution to manage the radio frequency spectrum.

The operations of Intelsat and Intersputnik, the two global satellite communications systems, also indicate the need for a strengthened IFRB. Although members of both of these bodies are also members of ITU, their frequency assignments are normally worked out by committees set up by the two organizations before the relevant information is passed to the IFRB.

The various international organizations and ITU must develop procedures for cooperation in the orderly recording and use of frequency assignments, and particularly the management of the spectrum.

To facilitate its work in the developing countries the IFRB also needs to arrange frequent study group meetings and coordination meetings similar to those undertaken by the other specialized secretariats of the International Telecommunication Union.

The board needs to increase its use of computer techniques so that it can keep all its records up to date, particularly the Master Frequency Register, for the various services that use the radio frequency spectrum.

From the final acts of the recent World Administrative Radio Conference for Space Telecommunications in Geneva in January 1967 the following matters which came under review go to stress the need for strengthening of the IFRB Secretariat:

- Revision of frequency allocations 1800 KHz to 275 GHz.

- Partial revision of the Radio Regulations, namely the Radio Regulations, Geneva 1959, as partially revised by the Extraordinary Administrative Radio Conference to allocate frequency hands for space radio-communication purposes, Geneva 1963, by the Extraordinary Administrative Radio Conference for the preparation of a revised allotment plan for the Aeronautical Mobile (R) Services, Geneva, 1966, and by the World Administrative Radio Conference to deal with matters relating to the Maritime Mobile Services, Geneva 1967.

- Revision of Article 9—Notification in the Master International Frequency Register of frequency assignments to terrestrial radio-communication stations.

- Notification of frequency assignments and coordination procedure to be applied in appropriate cases.

- Revision of Article 9(a)—Coordination, notification and recording in the Master International Frequency Register of frequency assignments to radio astronomy, space radio-communications stations, except stations in the broadcasting satellite services.

- Procedure for determination of the coordination area around the earth station in frequency bands between 1 and

40 GHz shared between space and terrestrial radio communication services.

- Recommendation relating to the examination by the World Administrative Conference of the situation with regard to occupation of the frequency spectrum in space radio-communications.
- Recommendation relating to technical standards for the assessment of harmful interference in the frequency bands above 28 MHz.

The present secretariat of the IFRB consists of five board members with supporting staff, with their duties defined under Article 13 of the International Telecommunication Convention, Montreux 1965; the structure of the IFRB secretariat is in need of a review. Such a review can only be put forward by member countries at the forthcoming Plenipotentiary Conference in Geneva, 1973.

The limits on utilization of the radio frequency spectrum have steadily risen from 30 MHz in 1927 to 60 MHz in 1932, 200 MHz in 1938, 10.5 GHz in 1947, 40 GHz in 1959, and 275 GHz at the last World Administrative Radio Conference. The tasks facing ITU as an international institution in the coordination and utilization of the radio frequency spectrum are formidable.

APPENDIX C

The International Telecommunication Union: ITU's Structure and Functions*

Harold K. Jacobson

I

The International Telecommunication Union (ITU), the oldest of the agencies of the United Nations family, traces its origins to the International Telegraph Convention signed in Paris in 1865. ITU has been in continuous existence since then, despite crises and even wars among its members.

That ITU is the most venerable of the UN agencies should hardly be surprising. In few fields is the need for international collaboration as obvious as it is in communications. Since about 1800, technological developments—first the telegraph, then the telephone, and then radio and television—have enhanced man's ability to transmit increasingly complex messages rapidly over long distances, and at substantially decreasing costs. Today, oral and visual messages transmitted through communications satellites can circle the globe in just a few seconds. But the globe is divided into sovereign states, and they must cooperate to reap the full benefits of this technological progress. National communications systems must be technically compatible with one

* Another version of this paper appears in *The International Law of Communications*, edited by Edward McWhinney, A. W. Sijthoff, Leyden, and Oceana Publications, Inc., Dobbs Ferry, New York, 1971.

another if they are to be interconnected, and since radio transmissions frequently cannot be confined within states, collaboration is necessary to avoid interference.

The obvious benefits of international collaboration have generally been compelling, and starting with the 1849 treaty between Austria and Prussia, providing for the linking of their telegraph lines, international cooperative arrangements have closely followed technological developments. It soon became apparent that multilateral, and potentially universal or quasi-universal, agreements would in most instances bring greater benefits than bilateral agreements; the first multilateral instruments were signed only a few years after the Austrian-Prussian treaty. The 1865 Conference in Paris, though, was a milestone, for it not only was attended by representatives of twenty states, including all of those that were then considered important in world politics, but also established an institutional framework to facilitate collaborative efforts—the International Telegraph Union.

Three years later, in another far-reaching step, the members of the union established a permanent bureau. Gradually the union expanded its functions. In 1885 it began to draft regulations for the telephone. It assumed further responsibilities at the Madrid Conference in 1932, when it merged with the International Radio Telegraph Union, which had been created in 1906. The Madrid Conference also gave the union its present name, the International Telecommunication Union, a modification which kept the acronym ITU unchanged.

Although ITU's existence is testimony to the virtual necessity of collaboration among states, the union and its history also reflect the desire of those states to retain maximum control over communications processes. Communications systems could have been organized on an international basis and ITU or some similar body given responsibility for their operation. Instead, communications systems have generally been organized within individual nations and operational responsibility has been assigned to national entities. Occasionally, groups of nations have joined together to organize and operate communications systems. Intelsat (the International Telecommunications Satellite Consortium) is the most comprehensive of these, but even it does not have universal membership. States have insisted on maintaining control of communications systems individually or sharing control only with friendly states, primarily because of the importance of such systems to the civilian and military functions of government. Governments feel that their ability to control their citizens and to pursue their chosen policies might be seriously jeopardized if they did not have control of their communications systems.

States have assigned to ITU only the functions of facilitating connections among systems and preventing these systems from interfering with one another. States have seen ITU not as an independent, decision-making agency but as a framework within which they could bargain among themselves. They have viewed the Secretariat mainly as a body that services conferences and have never been enthusiastic about building up either its powers or its staff. This has been true from the outset. The only controversial issue at the Paris Conference in 1865 was whether or not a permanent bureau was needed, and three years elapsed before the negative decision taken then was reversed.

From one standpoint, the unwillingness of states to assign more than the most limited functions to ITU may seem a serious liability. It has certainly served to constrain the union's growth. In another perspective, though, it may actually have been an asset, for had the union had more extensive functions, particularly in the operation of communications systems, it might not have been able to weather the many crises among its members that it has successfully withstood. ITU's limited role has served to insulate it from the ebb and flow of tensions in world politics.

The International Telecommunication Union's present mandate, as defined in the Convention negotiated at the Montreux Conference in 1965, is broadly "to maintain and extend international cooperation for the improvement and rational use of telecommunications of all kinds."[1] ITU is also charged with promoting "the development of technical facilities and their most efficient operation." More specifically, ITU's functions are to:

(a) effect allocation of the radio frequency spectrum and registration of radio frequency assignments;

[1] International Telecommunication Convention (Montreux, 1965), Art. 4, paragraph 2.

40

(b) coordinate efforts to eliminate harmful interference between radio stations of different countries and to improve the use made of the radio frequency spectrum;

(c) foster collaboration with respect to the establishment of the lowest possible rates;

(d) foster the creation, development and improvement of telecommunication equipment and networks in new or developing countries by every means at its disposal, especially its participation in the appropriate programs of the United Nations;

(e) promote the adoption of measures for ensuring the safety of life through the cooperation of telecommunication services;

(f) undertake studies, make regulations, adopt resolutions, formulate recommendations and opinions, and collect and publish information concerning telecommunications matters for the benefit of all Members and Associate Members.

Of these six functions, two, (b) and (d), were added when the Telecommunication Convention was revised in 1959 at the Geneva Conference; the others have been unchanged since the major revision of the Convention in 1947 at the Atlantic City Conference. All of them are fairly narrowly defined.

II

To perform these functions, the members of ITU have created a complex institutional structure. As determined by the Montreux Plenipotentiary Conference in 1965, ITU consists of: the Plenipotentiary Conference; Administrative Conferences; the Administrative Council; and the so-called permanent organs, including (a) the General Secretariat, (b) the International Frequency Registration Board (IFRB), (c) the International Radio Consultative Committee (CCIR) and (d) the International Telegraph and Telephone Consultative Committee (CCITT).

The Plenipotentiary Conference is the supreme organ of the International Telecommunication Union. It consists of delegations sent by all members and associate members. It meets at irregular intervals of five to eight years. Its most important functions are to determine ITU's general policies, to establish the basis for the budget and determine a fiscal limit for expenditures, and to

41

revise the Telecommunication Convention if it considers such revision necessary. In addition, it elects the Secretary-General, the Deputy Secretary-General and the members of ITU who serve on the Administrative Council.

The Administrative Council consists of twenty-nine members who meet annually and could meet more often. It oversees the administration of the union and in certain instances acts on behalf of the Plenipotentiary Conference.

Administrative Conferences—global or regional—are normally convened to consider specific telecommunication matters. Their principal function is the periodic partial or complete revision of the Telegraph Regulations, the Telephone Regulations, the Radio Regulations and the Additional Radio Regulations, which are collectively called the Administrative Regulations. In addition, World Administrative Conferences dealing with radio communication elect the five members of the International Frequency Registration Board. Although only member states have voting privileges in the Administrative Conferences, representatives of other international organizations and of recognized private operating agencies may also attend the sessions.

The International Consultative Committees study and issue recommendations concerning technical and operating questions. The CCIR and CCITT operate through *ad hoc* working parties, study groups, World and Regional Plan Committees, and Plenary Assemblies. Plenary Assemblies meet every three years. Only they can adopt formal recommendations; they also elect the directors of the CCIR and CCITT. Recognized private operating agencies and scientific and industrial organizations, as well as member states and associate member states of ITU, may participate in the work of the International Consultative Committees. Only ITU member states may vote in the Plenary Assemblies, but if a state is absent, the recognized private operating agencies of that country may, acting together, cast a single vote.

ITU's secretariat consists of four distinct parts, each of which is headed by one or more elected officials. The largest is the General Secretariat, with a staff of more than 250, directed by the Secretary-General and the Deputy Secretary-General. The International Frequency Registration Board is the second-largest component. Headed by its five elected members, the IFRB has a staff of about one hundred. The CCIR and the CCITT each have a staff of about twenty-five or thirty headed by an elected director. In all, ITU has nine elected officials and an appointed staff of over four hundred. The elected heads of each component of the secretariat are chosen by and work with slightly different constituencies which could impel them toward somewhat different orientations.

The Montreux Convention provided for a Coordination Committee consisting of the Secretary-General, the Deputy Secretary-General, the directors of the International Consultative Committees and the chairman of the International Frequency Registration Board. The Convention admonishes this committee to reach conclusions unanimously and allows the Secretary-General to act without the support of two or more of its members only in matters that he judges to be urgent. When the matter is not urgent, the Convention provides that it should be referred to the Administrative Council.

ITU's complex institutional structure is a result of its long history and evolution. As the union acquired new functions, new organs were grafted onto the previously existing structure. Such organs have by now gained a certain legitimacy and it is difficult to consider abolishing, amalgamating or even revising them. The complexity is also useful to states that are unwilling to grant substantial powers to the union. The presence of many elected officials who must refer their disagreements to the Administrative Council limits the autonomy of the Secretariat. Finally, complexity is compatible with the technical nature of ITU's activities. The present structure is designed to facilitate the participation of specialists in the consideration of technical questions, and it recognizes that specialists are not equally adept in all aspects of ITU's activities.

III

Facilitating connections among communications systems requires some standardization of operating and administrative procedures as well as of equipment. For this purpose the International Consultative Committees make recommendations covering a wide range of topics. For example, the Plenary Assembly of the CCITT in Mar del Plata, Argentina, in 1968, adopted recommendations on the issuance of credit cards to telecommunication users, a new international telegraph alphabet, specifications for echo suppressors and a host of other subjects. The recommendations adopted at the Plenary Assembly of an International Consultative Committee fill several volumes.

Study groups take the initial steps in framing recommendations which, however, can only be formally adopted by Plenary Assemblies. The recommendations are merely that; they have no binding power. Nevertheless, there is considerable incentive to comply with them, for only through compliance can connections among systems be made.

Frequently the recommendations of the International Consultative Committees have substantial financial implications. Local communications systems are usually designed with local conditions in mind and consequently vary from place to place. Connecting them can require modifications in one or more of the systems. The recommendations of the International Consultative Committees determine how the burdens of making modifications will be distributed. When new technology is involved, recommendations specifying standards may mean giving legitimacy to certain patient holders and not to others. Obviously, such recommendations can involve millions of dollars.

Because of both the non-binding character of recommendations and the substantial financial stakes involved, great efforts are made in the International Consultative Committees to achieve consensus and unanimity. Although majority voting is the formal rule in Plenary Assemblies, it is almost never invoked. Plenary Assemblies generally accept the conclusions of study groups with little or no modification. Although all members of the International Consultative Committees can participate in the study groups, usually only a few do. The participants in the study groups generally come from the states most advanced technically in the field of telecommunications—the United States, the Soviet Union, Japan, the United Kingdom, France, the Federal Republic of Germany, Canada, Czechoslovakia, Italy, Belgium and the Netherlands. The study groups proceed on the basis of technical papers. The participants have to be technically competent, and they are generally sophisticated about their colleagues' positions, problems and power. Their recommendations are the result of a process of mutual adjustment in which economic and technical costs are carefully weighed and apportioned. Influence varies with the issue being considered, but it is almost never distributed equally. For instance, it is extremely unlikely that a recommendation concerning telephones would be formulated without consideration for the interests of the United States, which has almost half the telephones in service in the world. Since the objective of participation in the International Consultative Committees is to communicate with others, the unequal distribution of influence in study groups seldom results in states' exercising veto powers. Rather it means that all participants will compromise, but some will compromise more than others.

The International Consultative Committees have formulated a tremendous number of recommendations, and compliance with them is very high. In only two instances have the committee members been unable to agree on recommendations. Both involved the CCIR, which proved unable to formulate recommendations concerning equipment specifications for black-and-white and color television. As a result, different television systems are now employed in different parts of the world, and the reception of programs transmitted from stations of one system by receivers designed for another is difficult. With these exceptions, however, the committee's record in obtaining agrement has been exceptionally good.

Despite this substantial achievement, ITU members and informed observers have leveled three criticisms against the International Consultative Committees. The first is that the process of formulating recommendations is too time-consuming, especially in view of the rapid pace of technological advance in the field of telecommunications. The process of mutual adjustment in study groups is slow, and recommendations can be adopted only at Plenary Assemblies, which meet every three years. Critics maintain that this time lag can restrain the production of equipment or result in the production of incompatible equipment. Defenders of the present system point out that almost all issues are technically complex and that mutual adjustment of interests is necessarily a slow process. They also assert that once a study group has reached a conclusion, its formal adoption by a Plenary Assembly can be taken for granted. Nevertheless, there seems to be growing sentiment within ITU for the adoption of procedures that would permit more rapid action when necessary.

The second criticism of the International Consultative Committees is that they pay insufficient attention to the problems and interests of ITU's less developed member states. This criticism is two-pronged. One charge is that the subjects considered are disproportionately those that primarily concern the developed states. The other is that the recommendations pay insufficient attention to the interests of the developing countries. (Since the recommendations frequently involve systems with several variables, many trade-offs are possible, for instance between cost and versatility. The interests of states in these trade-offs may vary, depending on, among other things, their level of economic development.)

The merit of this criticism is difficult to judge. In certain instances the most advanced technology may be more economical for less developed than for highly developed states, given the heavy investment of the latter in existing equipment. In any case, it is not difficult to understand why the processes of the International Consultative Committees could leave ITU's less developed members uneasy. Inputs come almost exclusively from highly developed states, and bargains are struck among their representatives. The small staffs of the two CCI's can hardly do more than provide the necessary administrative services for meetings.

Few changes to alter this situation are realistically possible. The work of the International Consultative Committees depends on a high level of technical expertise. The repositories of such expertise are the manufacturers of telecommunication equipment and the operators of major telecommunication systems, both located mainly in the developed countries of the world. Furthermore, the facts that almost half of the telephones in service in the world are located in the United States and that communications occur predominantly among the developed states of the Atlantic area, Oceania and Japan are unlikely to change quickly. However, if the CCI's staffs had more extensive technical resources, they might contribute to the work of the committees inputs less colored by the interests of the developed states.

The third criticism of the International Consultative Committees is that they treat radio communications and telegraph and telephone communications separately. Although at one time the technology of telegraphy and telephony was quite separate from that of radio, increasingly the two have blended together. Communications satellites, for example, which rely on radio for transmission from ground stations to the satellite and back again to ground stations carry telegraph and telephone as well as radio and television traffic. The two CCIs have dealt with problems stemming from the merger of the technologies by establishing joint bodies, but in some areas the work of the two committees overlaps and in others neither is competent. One wonders if it would not be more efficient to merge the two CCIs.

The elaboration of standards which are of a more fundamental and permanent nature than those treated by the recommendations of the International Consultative Committees is dealt with by ITU through the Administrative Regulations, which are revised by Administrative Conferences. The present Administrative Regulations are products of long evolution, some provisions dating from the union's earliest days. The Telegraph Regulations and the Telephone Regulations were revised most recently in 1958, and the Radio Regulations and Additional Radio Regulations in 1959, with further partial revisions in 1963 and 1971 (dealing with space), in 1966 (dealing with aeronautical services) and in 1967 (dealing with maritime services).

The Administrative Regulations are adopted by a majority of those present and voting in Administrative Conferences. Article 15 of the International Telecommunication Convention states that ratification of the Convention involves "acceptance" of the Administrative Regulations in force at the time of ratification or accession. The same article obliges members to inform the Secretary-General of ITU of their approval of any revision of these regulations. The regulations are binding on those states that have approved them, but generally there is no mechanism for enforcement other than the permission granted to states not to apply certain provisions, particularly those relating to rates in the case of states which themselves do not apply these provisions. In other words, retaliation is permissible. However, the vast majority of ITU members approve the periodic revisions of the Administrative Regulations, and even those that do not tend to apply most of their provisions. Again, the desire to communicate is a powerful incentive to compliance.

To this point attention has been focused on those of ITU's traditional functions relating to facilitating connections among systems. Another traditional function, partially discharged through the Administrative Regulations, is making arrangements to prevent interference between communications systems. Stations transmitting on the same radio frequency can under certain circumstances interfere with one another and make reception of their signals difficult or impossible. All systems that rely completely or partly on the transmission through air of electric waves—radio and television, obviously, but also some telegraph and telephone systems—run this risk. States have given ITU several functions intended to prevent such interference.

First, ITU is charged with the allocation of the radio frequency spectrum. Administrative Conferences allocate certain frequency bands for specific purposes such as maritime mobile, broadcasting, aeronautical radio navigation, land mobile, amateur and space. Some allocations are made on a global basis, others vary among three regions. Roughly, Region I consists of Western Europe, Africa, the USSR and Mongolia; Region II, the Americas; and Region III, the remainder of Asia and Oceania. Additional distinctions are made for the tropical zone, a band which varies slightly with the three regions but which roughly includes the area between the parallels 30 degrees north and 35 degrees south. The allocations agreed to in the Administrative Conference are embodied in the Radio Regulations.

Assignment to stations or users of specific frequencies within these allocations is the responsibility of member states. In the United States, for instance, the Federal Communications Commission makes frequency assignments. The Radio Regulations require members to report to the International Frequency Registration Board (IFRB) all assignments that are to be used for international radio communication, that might cause harmful interference with services of other states or for which international recognition is desired. The board then notifies all member states of this assignment and checks to see if it conforms with the Telecommunication Convention and the Table of Frequency Allocations or is likely to cause harmful interference with a frequency assignment already recorded in its Master Register. If the board's findings are favorable, the assignment will be recorded in the Master Register as of the date of receipt. The board receives an average of more than 1,700 assignments each week and gives favorable findings in at least 70 percent of them.

If the board finds that the assignment is likely to cause harmful interference, it returns the notice to the authority that made the assignment with its findings and perhaps suggestions for a solution. If a state insists on maintaining a frequency assignment despite an unfavorable finding by the board, it may nonetheless gain recognition for the assignment, for the regulations provide that if an assignment has been in use for at least sixty days without the board's receiving a complaint of harmful interference the assignment shall be recorded in the Master Register.

If assignments are not brought into use within 120 days after they are reported to the board, the board may cancel the entry in the Master Register. The board may also cancel or alter entries if the use of an assignment has been discontinued or does not accord with the basic characteristics specified in the notification, but only with the agreement of the notifying administration.

Once an assignment is entered in the Master Register, it has international recognition and a certain legitimacy. It is generally in all parties' interest to avoid harmful interference, and there is little to be gained by ignoring entries on the Master Register. However, if a party wilfully ignores them, ITU has no power to impose sanctions. States can report cases of harmful interference to the IFRB but the most that the board can do is to study the problem and suggest possible ways of solving it. The Radio Regulations leave the solution of the problem to the conflicting parties, merely admonishing them to act in good faith.

Although the IFRB's powers have never been more extensive than they now are, when it was first created at the Atlantic City Conference in 1947 a number of Americans who were principally responsible for its creation hoped that it would enter, even with its modest powers, into the field of frequency management. They saw it as something of a cross between the Federal Communications Commission and the International Court of Justice. Several states, particularly the Soviet Union, never agreed with this conception, and in practice the board has fallen far short of it.

According to the 1947 revision of the Telecommunication Convention, the board could take the initiative in furnishing advice to members "with a view to the operation of the maximum practicable number of radio channels in those positions of the spectrum where harmful interference may occur."[2] For a variety of reasons the board has not developed this role extensively, although the provision has remained in the Convention. Nor has it developed extensively a mediatory role in cases of harmful interference.

How adequate ITU's system of frequency allocation and registration is to modern communications needs is a matter of controversy. Many maintain that the system is as good as can reasonably be expected, given the basic desire of states to retain control over their communications facilities. Others are critical. Representatives of both developed and less developed states have attacked the system of frequency allocation by Administrative Conferences. Those from developed countries distrust voting as a way of settling such matters and are disdainful of the technical competence of some participants. Those from developing countries, on the other hand, feel overpowered by the developed countries with their immense technical resources.

If pressed, however, neither side in this controversy can point to substantial specific needs that have been ignored in the frequency allocation process. Furthermore, it is hard to conceive of a fundamentally different system that would be widely accepted. There is little evidence that states would be willing to turn such a sensitive matter over to a group of experts or a small council of governmental representatives. The present system does give each state a voice, and some, because of their greater technical resources, gain greater influence.

Both groups, however, have raised less sweeping issues. Some economists and engineers from developed states have argued that the present system of frequency allocation is too rigid and consequently inefficient, wasteful and ill-adapted to a field where technological progress is extremely rapid. They maintain that once an allocation has been made it is seldom changed, and that, since many services are quite local, allocations need not cover areas as large as the three regions, much less the globe. In their

[2] International Telecommunication Convention (Atlantic City, 1947), Art. 6.

view the present system places greater pressure on certain portions of the spectrum and underutilizes other portions. They would like to see greater flexibility. One argument against flexibility is that enterprises might be reluctant to undertake the heavy capital investment often required to develop a radio communication system, if they felt that within a short time the system would have to be altered to take account of new allocations. Still, some midpoint might be found which would allow greater flexibility and room for experimentation than the present system and still not inhibit investment or, worse yet, invite chaos.

Some government officials from less developed states maintain that the present system is mainly responsive to those states that have the technical resources to foresee and express their needs—that is, the developed states. These officials fear that their needs, which they may have difficulty foreseeing, will be slighted. Similar fears have also been expressed by user groups such as radio astronomers, who are ordinarily not well represented in state delegations to ITU conferences. One way of altering the situation somewhat might be to build up the technical competence of ITU's staff so that it would make a greater substantive contribution in ITU conferences. Being responsible only to the union, it would be relatively disinterested and in a position to present broad public interest concerns. ITU staff work could serve to supplement the technical resources of the less developed countries. Decisions, of course, would continue to be made by states. The purpose of the change would be to work toward making all relevant information available before decisions were made and to strengthen the position of some of the weaker participants. Greater flexibility in allocations might also help.

Most radio stations are registered with the International Frequency Registration Board. Some, however, are not, and some do not even operate within the proper allocations. The board can do nothing about them. Clearly states have not so far felt that this problem is serious enough to warrant taking steps through ITU to alter it, and in certain areas of application, at least, it is unlikely that this attitude will soon change. Article 51 of the Telecommunication Convention explicitly states that "Members and Associate Members retain their entire freedom with regard to military radio installations of their army, naval and air forces."[3] In the realm of civilian activities, however, increasing use of the frequency spectrum may make states more willing to take steps against users who contravene ITU regulations. Short of giving ITU power to impose sanctions—a most unlikely prospect—members can take some measures to discourage illicit use of the frequency spectrum. For instance, the IFRB or ITU staff could be given the power to monitor spectrum usage and publish the findings. Present arrangements allow only national administrations to conduct monitoring activities. The change would be a modest one, but it might slightly inhibit illegal users.

ITU's newer tasks, relating to the provision of assistance to developing countries, can be described in more precise terms than its traditional functions. In its annual summary of its activities for 1970, for instance, the union reported that it had, "through its various programs of technical cooperation, provided assistance to developing countries for a total value of U.S. $6,050,-198 in the form of 241 expert missions, 395 fellowships implemented or under implementation and U.S. $780,187 equipment delivered."[4] The broad goals of these activities were: (a) to promote the development of telecommunication networks in Africa, Asia and Latin America; (b) to strengthen telecommunication services in developing countries; and (c) to develop the human resources required for telecommunication. None of these activities are financed from ITU's regular budget; the bulk of the funds come from the United Nations Development Program.

Evaluating ITU's performance of these newer functions, though, is as difficult as in the case of the traditional functions. One issue is the quantitative adequacy of ITU's activities. At the Montreux Conference some representatives of less developed states proposed that ITU begin financing technical cooperation activities from its own budget, but the developed states successfully opposed this proposal, arguing that its adoption would give telecommunications a priority in development. They maintained that UNDP financing is preferable because it covers all aspects of development and hence forces recipients to weight telecommunications needs against others. UNDP funding procedures,

[3] International Telecommunication Convention (Montreux, 1965), Art. 51.
[4] International Telecommunication Union, *Report on the Activities of the International Telecommunication Union in 1970*, Geneva, 1971, p. 36.

however, are complicated, take time, and tend to result in a relatively unchanging allocation among the various specialized agencies over the years. Moreover, UNDP funds must be allocated to specific projects. As a consequence, ITU can neither respond quickly to special needs nor engage in broad planning activities, and its technical assistance program can only grow proportionately with increases in over-all UNDP funding.

Another issue is how well ITU performs its technical assistance activities. No attempt has been made to compare ITU's efforts carefully with similar efforts conducted by individual governments of developed states or private companies. Impressionistic reports have been both favorable and unfavorable. ITU training enterprises have been described as more innovative and lively than those that were run under colonial rule by metropolitan powers and as less efficient than those managed by commercial enterprises. Clearly, this subject needs further investigation. One point, however, can be made. ITU staff members engaged in technical cooperation activities rarely interact with those engaged in the union's more traditional functions. Of course their tasks are different, but greater interaction could conceivably lead to the formulation of more innovative projects, some of which might have an impact on the feelings of developing states about the union's traditional functions and the conduct of these states in their functions.

This absence of interaction is not atypical of ITU's functioning. No other specialized agency of the United Nations has as complex a structure as ITU. How this structure arose is clear; whether it needs to persist is not. It undoubtedly allows special needs to be met in special ways by specialists. But perhaps a more unified structure could still serve this purpose. Structures, of course, are much less important than the quality of the individuals who fill the posts; good personnel can always surmount awkward structures. ITU's present structure, however, with its elaborate division of authority, is almost an invitation to bickering about picayune matters and may well discourage able personnel from association with the union. It also tends to compartmentalize the consideration of problems. This compartmentalization may have been appropriate when telegraph, telephone and radio were really quite different, but modern technological developments have made telecommunication systems more and more similar and interdependent. Wholistic treatment is clearly required. Joint groups have been created in ITU, but perhaps the time has arrived for even more far-reaching moves toward unity.

IV

ITU's next Plenipotentiary Conference is scheduled for 1973. The question of institutional reform will surely arise. This issue was raised at the Montreux Conference in 1965, but led only to the appointment of a study group to prepare a draft constitutional charter. This study group interpreted its mandate as being limited to recommending which sections of the Telecommunication Convention should be placed in a constitution that would be permanent and subject to amendment only by special procedure rather than by majority vote at each Plenipotentiary Conference, and which sections should be placed in General Regulations that would continue to be subject to revision at Plenipotentiary Conferences.

But the 1973 conference could be crucially important to ITU. If a constitution were adopted, it would no longer be possible to reconsider ITU's basic mandate and institutional structure at each Plenipotentiary Conference. Undoubtedly this change would ease the burden of these conferences. But it also could mean that ITU's mandate and structure would be firmly set for some years to come, for the experience of the United Nations and the specialized agencies indicates that constitutions are seldom amended and when they are the changes are minor. With all its disadvantages ITU's present system of reconsidering the entire Telecommunication Convention at each Plenipoteniary Conference may allow greater flexibility.

If this potential for flexibility is to be renounced, then it is incumbent on all participants in the 1973 conference to consider not only how well ITU has performed its functions in the past but also how adequate the union is to the needs of the future. Clearly the demand for telecommunication facilities will increase. Communications satellites have opened vast new technological possibilities. At the same time, the less developed states are strongly interested in the rapid development of their economies, and this will involve increased telecommunication facilities. Normal growth in established sectors plus demands stemming from these newer sources are bound to put increased demands on the union. Perhaps ITU's present institutions are adequate to meet these demands, but it is not unreasonable to suggest that as the union approaches the twenty-first century, it may need to shed, streamline, modernize and supplement its inheritance from the nineteenth and early twentieth centuries.

Today ITU's functions are more vital than when the union was created more than a century ago, and much more complex. The absolute amount of telecommunications and the rate of technological change have increased enormously. For this reason states may well need to reconsider their basic attitudes toward the union, particularly whether the union, apart from its technical assistance activities, should be seen principally as a framework within which they can settle matters among themselves by bargaining. No one has suggested that the union should itself undertake the operation of telecommunication systems or gain coercive powers over states. But several informed observers have questioned the value of confining the Secretariat's role to servicing conferences. It is with respect to this issue that serious discussion is needed. Equally serious consideration must be given to the matter of ITU's keeping pace with technological change. Modes of handling problems adopted in an era of less rapid technological change need to be reconsidered and thought needs to be given to building greater flexibility into ITU's procedures.

In 1865 the states assembled at Paris took a creative and far-reaching step when they formed the International Telegraph Union. That action has enormously facilitated communications among states in the succeeding century. Creative action is required now to facilitate continued progress.

APPENDIX D

Observations on the World Administrative Radio Conference for Space Telecommunications (WARC-ST) Geneva, June–July, 1971

Edward W. Ploman

Background and proceedings

In 1963 ITU convened an administrative radio conference that made the first limited frequency allocations to space communications services.

The rapid technical advances since 1963 have given a much clearer idea of the possibilities offered by space techniques and have made it necessary to provide a new framework of regulations for services that use or will use satellites. Satellite telecommunication and meteorology services are already in operation, and satellite broadcasting, earth resources surveying mobile services (i.e., for navigation and traffic control in the maritime and aerospace services) are expected to be introduced shortly. The growth of importance of space services can be assessed not only in terms of the number of new services but also in terms of the number of participants—some 700 delegates from 101 countries—in the 1971 conference.

The national delegations varied in size from one or two delegates to over seventy, most of whom represented the telecommunication administrations of their respective nations, assisted, in the large delegations, by experts from other areas such as meteorology, broadcasting, defense, space sciences, air traffic authorities, etc.

Mr. Gunnar Pedersen, Director-General of the Danish administration was elected chairman of the conference with Mr. Baladov of the Soviet Union and Mr. Tyson of the United States as vice-chairmen.

At the outset seven committees were established. These committees set up working groups and other groups most of which were divided into still smaller groups. Since many of these groups met at the same time, smaller delegations found it difficult to participate fully in the work of the conference. This question was in fact raised on a number of occasions, particularly by delegations from developing nations. On many occasions, the main substantive work was carried out by a surprisingly small number of delegations, although remarks and objections by others were taken into account to the point that any one delegation could jeopardize or hold up the entire proceedings.

The conference based its work on proposals submitted by administrations and on reports from ITU's permanent bodies, specifically the CCIR and its so-called Joint Special Meeting, which took place in January and February of this year.

Documentation at the conference was massive. The main series of documents numbered well above 400 items and was supplemented by other papers for the working subgroups. After discussion in the subgroups, the various questions were passed to the working groups, then taken up by the committees and, after passage through the Editorial Committee, discussed by the conference in plenary session.

Result of the conference

In accordance with the usual procedures of the ITU and such administrative conferences, the results of the WARC were set forth as "final acts," which are signed by the participating delegations and subject to approval by the members of ITU. Some of these final acts are revisions of the Radio Regulations that will enter into force on Januray 1, 1973, and be binding on the ITU members; others are resolutions and recommendations.

Assessing the results of the WARC is difficult, largely because the final acts, like the Radio Regulations themselves, intersperse important general questions with detailed technical calculations and minor administrative issues. Rather than attempt to address each point raised in the conference, this paper will deal with a few issues of particular relevance to broadcasters and with general or legal considerations.

Frequency Allocations

The conference allocated a number of frequency bands for various space radio-communication services, subject to a number of limitations and constraints regarding technical characteristics, notification, registration and coordination procedures and to so-called footnotes indicating in which countries the frequency bands are used for other purposes. The allocations finally agreed upon represent the outcome of negotiations and compromises—or, in certain cases, lack of compromise—with regard to the claims of different terrestrial and space services, the interests or fears of administrations, manufacturers or present users, differences in technological development and, often, a general unwillingness to abandon outdated practices and previously allocated frequency bands, whether actually used or not.

The allocations for fixed satellite service for television as well as sound radio include both the point-to-point communications and the so-called distribution satellite service (which does not figure as a defined category), special new allocations have been made for satellite broadcasting. Details of these allocations are to be found in the final acts of the conference but, subject to the constraints mentioned above, the following frequency bands have been allocated to the broadcast satellite service:

MHz 470- 890	Region 2[1]	on a shared basis with other space services
MHz 582- 606	Region 1	(fixed, mobile, radio-navigation)
MHz 606- 790	Region 1	
MHz 610- 942	Region 3	
MHz 2500-2690	Regions 1-3	on a shared basis with the provision that the use of this band by the broadcast satellite service is limited to domestic and regional systems for community reception and such use is subject to agreement among the administrations concerned. (The same provisions are also adopted for the fixed satellite service in this band.)
GHz 11.7- 12.5	Regions 1-3	on a shared basis (fixed, mobile terrestrial broadcasting) with the provision that existing and future fixed, mobile and broadcasting services shall not cause harmful inter-

ference to broadcast satellite stations
operating in accordance with the decisions of
the appropriate broadcasting frequency
assignment planning conference (see below).

GHz	22.5- 23	Region 3	on a shared basis
GHz	41- 43	Regions 1-3	on an exclusive basis
GHz	84- 86	Regions 1-3	on an exclusive basis

[1] Note on regions: For purposes of frequency allocation the world has been divided into three regions: Region 1 comprises Europe and Africa, including Turkey, the entire territory of the USSR and Mongolia; Region 2 comprises the Americas and Greenland; Region 3 comprises Asia and the Pacific except the Asian part of the USSR and Mongolia.

Regulations

The conference adopted a number of regulatory administrative and technical provisions. The administrative provisions are complex and difficult to interpret. The most important of them are:

- Complete revision of Article 9A of the Radio Regulations dealing with "Coordination, Notification, and Recording in the Master International Frequency Register of Frequency Assignments to Radio Astronomy and Space Radiocommunication Stations except Stations in the Broadcasting Satellite Service"; the revised article accompanied by a series of appendixes concerning form of notices, characteristics to be furnished, advance publication information to be furnished for a satellite network, etc.

- A special resolution (Spa G) concerning procedures "Relating to the Bringing into use of Broadcasting Space Stations, prior to the entry into force of Agreements and Associated Plans for the Broadcasting Satellite Service." (see below)

The technical provisions concern such matters as procedures for determining down to the last horizon elevation angle the coordination area around an earth station in frequency bands between 1 and 40 GHz shared between space and terrestrial radiocommunication services; methods of calculating the degree of interference between geostationary satellite networks sharing the same frequency bands, etc. These provisions seem more appropriate for publication in a technical handbook than for inclusion in an international convention with treaty force regulating the conduct of states.

Some of the adopted resolutions and recommendations are of a more general nature or include provisions for future action.

Equal rights. Resolution Spa D "Relating to the Use by All Countries, with Equal Rights, of Frequency Bands for Space Radio-communication Services" states:

That all countries have equal rights in the use of both the radio frequencies allocated to various space radio-communication services and the geostationary satellite orbit for these services [and] that the radio frequency spectrum and the geostationary orbit are limited natural resources and should be most effectively and economically used.

[Therefore] the registration with the ITU of frequency assignments for space radio-communication services and their use should not provide any permanent priority for any individual country or groups of countries and should not create an obstacle to the establishment of space systems by other countries, and that countries or groups of countries having registered frequencies with the ITU should take all practicable measures to realize the possibility of the use of new space systems by other countries.

These provisions seem consistent with the provisions of the Outer Space Treaty and the resolutions adopted by the UN General Assembly, although reference to activities outside telecommunication was singularly absent from the WARC discussions. They may help to safeguard the developing countries, which may someday wish to establish their own systems, from finding both the frequency spectrum and the geostationary orbit completely pre-empted.

Plans for the broadcasting satellite service. After long and arduous discussions, the conference adopted a resolution "Relating to the Establishment of Agreements and Associated Plans for the Broadcasting Satellite Service." It stated:

That stations in the broadcasting satellite service shall be established and operated in accordance with agreements and associated plans adopted by world or regional administrative conferences, as the case may be, in which all the administrations concerned, and the administrations whose services are liable to be affected may participate; that the Administrative Council be requested to examine as soon as possible the question of a world administrative conference, and/or regional administrative conferences as required, with a view to fixing suitable dates, places and agenda; that during the period before the entry into force of such agreements and associated plans the administrations and the IFRB shall apply the procedure contained in Resolution No. Spa G.

By establishing an interim procedure for broadcast satellite systems the conference has permitted satellite broadcasting systems to be set up before any plans are adopted. In view of the divergent opinions regarding the desirability of such plans, the resolution is more important than it seems.

Spillover. A number of proposals were made to the conference concerning political, social and other criteria with regard to the content of satellite broadcasts that can be received in countries other than those where the broadcast originates. Such matters clearly fall outside of ITU's competence and were not included in the final acts. But the conference did add to Article 7 of the Radio Regulations a new regulation (428 A) that states:

In devising the characteristics of a broadcasting space station, all technical means available shall be used to reduce, to the maximum extent practicable, the radiation over the territory of other countries unless an agreement has been previously reached with such countries.

This provision is couched in terms of technical characteristics and does not refer to content. (The UN Working Group on Direct Broadcast Satellites, in its reports which have been adopted by the Outer Space Committee and the General Assembly, has dealt with this matter in terms which seem more flexible.)

General Remarks

Although some of the following observations may seem unduly harsh, they are not intended to negate ITU's valuable work. Their purpose is to evaluate the principles, structures and procedures that the international community and individual countries have adopted in the increasingly important and complex field of telecommunications.

The WARC itself has many features that appear strange compared with the principles and procedures applied in other international contexts. A conference of this magnitude and importance could reasonably be expected to provide, through appropriate documentation and debate, general guidelines for its own work as well as for the future. Very few countries, however, gave any indication of the policy or reasons underlying their proposals. The conference participants did not engage in a general debate that could have provided directives for the work. Instead, they immediately split up in committees, working groups and subgroups; questions of principle and policy, such as the competence of the conference or the validity of its decisions, kept coming up in contexts where they could not be dealt with properly.

The failure of the participants to distinguish matters of principle from technical or administrative details was reflected not only in the discussions at the conference but also in the formulation of decisions and the content of documents. These weaknesses are characteristic of ITU and have serious implications. The Radio Regulations, for example, are almost impenetrably obscure to readers not already conversant with ITU and its work.

Furthermore, the inclusion of technical details in legally binding instruments which are revised only at irregular intervals makes technical innovation difficult; many administrations refuse to be bound by CCIR recommendations and will accept only decisions made by an Administrative Conference.

ITU member-countries vary widely in expertise, number of delegates and amount of preparatory work for the conference. These variations made themselves felt in the meetings. A few highly developed countries directed most of the work, while individual delegations provided what could be called obstruction, sometimes due purely to technical ignorance. The constitutional weakness of the central ITU bodies seems to make it impossible for them to question or reject positions of delegations even if they are patently wrong from a technical point of view. Moreover, little attention was paid to input from sources other than the delegates. Views presented by other international organizations, whether governmental or nongovernmental, seem to be given at best a grudging reception and no real importance.

The shortcomings of a conference like the WARC—and by implication of the ITU itself—should ultimately be imputed to the ITU members themselves. Although, in principle, ITU's membership consists of national governments, its work is carried out almost exclusively by telecommunications administrations without much reference to governments or their positions in other contexts. The WARC functioned as a conference of administrations taking, on behalf of their governments, positions that were not based, in most cases, on a firm, coherent national communications policy. In a field in which the majority of countries have no coherent national policy it is obviously difficult to achieve a coherent international policy.

The weakness of ITU's central bodies, moreover, results from the almost obsessive insistence of ITU members on an exclusive, narrow vision of national sovereignty, often in glaring contradiction to the attitudes of other international organizations and the actual multinational, commercial policies of telecommunication industries. Many countries which in other contexts have accepted, to a large extent, such modern concepts of international behavior and international law as the interdependence of nations, mutuality of interests, common objectives, far-reaching international cooperation, have not done so within the ITU context. Compared to the Outer Space Treaty, the Radio Regulations—even those dealing exclusively with space communications—are based on concepts that are outdated by a century or more.

It became quite clear during the WARC that there are no general principles or internationally accepted rules regarding the legal status of frequency allocations and attendant regulations. International commitments made by governments through their telecommunications administrations within the ITU seem to have a different character than commitments accepted in other contexts.

Conclusions

Analysis of the WARC leads to the conclusion that basic principles of international cooperation in the telecommunication field have yet to be established. Once they have been formulated in a manner that corresponds to the present-day goals and needs of the international community, ITU's structure and procedures can be worked out in detail.

The ITU Plenipotentiary Conference in 1973 will provide an opportunity to deal with these questions. The Plenipotentiary Conference is the only ITU body empowered to change or revise the International Telecommunication Convention and to adopt general principles. Telecommunications administrations cannot be expected to change their basic attitudes. Governments, which in most cases seem unaware of both the importance and short-comings of the ITU and of the activities of their administrations, will probably be active only to a limited degree. Other intergovernmental organizations are unlikely to do more than look into working methods and organization within the context of present conventions and rules.

The only plausible source of innovation is the independent national and international organizations. It is strongly recommended that they undertake to formulate some basic principles of international cooperation in the telecommunication field. These principles should ultimately serve as the basis of a proposal for an ITU Charter which would combine relevant aspects of both the Convention and the Radio Regulations.

This work could usefully be undertaken by such bodies as the International Broadcast Institute, in cooperation or consultation with or assisted by appropriate national bodies or individuals. The resulting proposals should be communicated to governments, through such channels as the ministries of foreign affairs, to other interested and relevant institutions, particularly those with influence in these areas, and to interested individuals.

Timing is of great importance. Since proposals have to be submitted by ITU members some four to six months before the conference, which is expected to take place in September–October 1973, and since governments would need at least some months to study and decide on proposals for the revision of the ITU Convention, the work recommended here must be finished by the end of 1972.

APPENDIX E

The International Telecommunication Union: Its Functions and Structure

Jean Voge

ITU's essential task is "to coordinate, harmonize, and regulate international communications." The union must also promote the future development of the global telecommunications network with a maximum of efficiency in both technology and resource utilization (the resources, in the case of the frequency spectrum and sometimes, too, the location of telecommunications installations, are limited), economy and fairness to the user nations, developed or developing. These requirements are often contradictory. For example, the use of wide frequency band modulations can reduce the power requirements and therefore also the cost of transmitters, but wide bands consume more of the frequency spectrum. The most economical design for the world as a whole—for example, large earth stations for satellite communications—may impose special burdens on countries with little communications traffic. Cable links, even when they are more expensive than radio links, may be preferable or even necessary to prevent interference and to compensate for what in certain regions might be described as total saturation of the radio spectrum. This situation already prevails, for example, in television broadcasting and short wave communications.

To be sure, users of many communications services will have the freedom to select locations and installation characteristics—subject to certain restrictions imposed by ITU regulations or plans in force. But the growth in demand for telecommunications and the development of an increasingly complex and overlapping global network, composed of systems which must be jointly undertaken and shared by numerous users (as in the case of satellites), will inevitably result in less freedom and more abandonment of national sovereignty for the benefit of the international community. The number of partners involved in coordination procedures will grow very rapidly. Disputes concerning interference will be more and more frequent and difficult to solve. Only ITU can provide a framework and the means necessary for the solution of these problems. Only ITU has the data and the independence required to study and recommend a true optimization of all parameters involved at the global level, and not only to make rules but also, eventually, to deliver final judgments in cases of persistent conflict among users of the global network.

Functions and activities of ITU

ITU's regulations concerning international telecommunications appear in the International Telecommunication Convention drawn up by Plenipotentiary Conferences, and the Radio Regulations and Telephone and Telegraph Regulations, drawn up by Administrative Conferences. Over the years the Telephone and Telegraph Regulations seem to have fallen into disuse and are being replaced by simple recommendations made by the CCITT. The 1971 Space Conference adopted a resolution empowering the CCIR to make recommendations modifying the technical criteria included in the Radio Regulations for the sharing of frequency bands. The committee will consult with governments and those that accept its recommendations within four months will be able to use the new criteria rather than those originally provided for in the Radio Regulations. This procedure should permit the Radio Regulations to respond more flexibly to technological advances.

We agree with the proposal of the Panel of the American Society of International Law that ITU establish a high level working group on codification, responsible for making the regulations simpler, clearer and more coherent.[1] This group would prepare a draft for approval by an Administrative Conference. Alternatively, the ITU Secretariat could undertake this task and submit its draft to the ITU membership. Revision of the regulations ought to include distinguishing clearly between fundamental principles and the necessarily more complex details of application.

The IFRB is in charge of administering frequency assignments and preventing radio interference. A national telecommunications administration may apply for a recommendation from the IFRB if it wishes to operate a transmitter or represents a group of nations that want to establish a joint communications satellite system. The applicant is bound to observe the ITU regulatory norms and to coordinate its radio communications with those of all affected administrations. Ultimately the IFRB issues a sort of judgment as to whether the regulations have been observed and as to the risk of harmful interference with previously approved stations. If the finding is unfavorable, the board defers approval of the assignment, giving the applicant the time and opportunity to revise the proposed system in order to render it acceptable.

The IFRB lacks the power of final decision and must accept an assignment, even if it has issued an unfavorable finding, if no interference is found within four months after the station is put into operation. But at least in the field of space communications since the 1971 Space Conference, unapproved assignments remain somewhat tentative. If they should subsequently cause interference to a station that had received its assignment previously, or even subsequently but with an entirely favorable IFRB finding, the administration responsible must put an immediate end to the interference. The IFRB can also cancel any assignment that has not been used for the last two years.

With the increasing saturation of the spectrum the danger of interference will become progressively greater and the above procedures may become inapplicable. In accordance with a resolution of the Space Conference, the ITU Administrative Council may, prior to accepting definitive assignments for satellite broadcasting, convene a special planning conference like those that have

[1] *The International Telecommunication Union: Issues and Next Steps,* A Report by the Panel on International Telecommunications Policy of the American Society of International Law, Occasional Paper No. 10, Carnegie Endowment for International Peace, June 1971, pp. 24–25.

been held in the past, particularly in the field of radio broadcasting.

In certain cases the IFRB could also deliver genuine judgments, if the independence of the judges were strengthened. In making these judgments, the board would have to take into account not only the problems of interference but also such possible alternative solutions as cable or radio. This change would require ITU to undertake real over-all planning.

The CCIR and CCITT set technical standards and conduct research on technical advances and their application. These activities result in a proliferation of documents: recommendations at the final stage, reports in the case of information data, and preliminary conclusions on the subject during the course of the study. But like the regulations the publications are often too voluminous for users and it is rather difficult to keep up with them. The material needs pruning and restructuring—work that could be done by the secretariats. Moreover, except for the few questions for study that are raised by, for example, the IFRB, projects are most often selected by the assemblies of the International Consultative Committees. On the one hand, these issues may not always be the most important from a general point of view. On the other hand, they tend to duplicate the efforts of other scientific organizations.

The subcommittee meetings are so numerous that only very large countries are able to present documents and send participants to all of them.

The secretariats of the CCIR and of the CCITT play very different roles. The secretariat of the CCIR does not perform any preliminary work of analysis or synthesis; everything is done by the delegates to the assemblies, whereas the CCITT secretariat appears to play a role of prime importance in the drafting of the final texts.

The Consultative Committees should clearly constitute the technical organs of ITU and, in addition to their own work, should assist other departments (IFRB, Technical Assistance, Planning Organ, if one is created). Such cooperation would represent an orientation toward optimization of the global telecommunications system as a whole, rather than merely towards this or that particular type of equipment. The other departments of

ITU might then substantially increase the number of questions they put to the Consultative Committees and their work would be more realistic and effective. Moreover, the Radio and Telephone/telegraph Committees could be more or less combined, since the two types of communications media, cable and radio, would be increasingly interconnected and, depending on circumstances, used alternatively.

The secretariats also could play a more important preparatory role for the meetings by analyzing and synthesizing the proposals received, and presenting them impartially. This procedure would reduce the work of the delegates and hence the length of the meetings. The secretariats should be able to put the texts adopted into final form and to summarize them, making them easier for the members to use. The increases in manpower and in the budget of the secretariats that these changes would require could be largely offset by cuts in the personnel and costs of the general assemblies.

Finally, the secretariats should offer to conduct, for countries that do not have the means of undertaking them, studies geared to the special circumstances of such countries at the committees' expense. The secretariats might also hire more staff members from the developing countries.

Planning

Today no ITU organ is specifically charged with planning, although within the framework of the Consultative Committees world and regional plan committees have been created. Various Administrative Conferences have functioned as planning conferences, particularly in the field of radio broadcasting. Although the 1971 Space Conference made provision for planning conferences for satellite broadcasting, it perceived the need for short-term planning for all of space communications. The relevant coordination procedures are to be preceded by publication of the characteristics of the projects, as early as five years before they are to become operational, and by inquiries addressed to national telecommunications administrations. The ensuing discussions might eventually lead to a modification of already existing networks of systems.

We believe that some long-term planning would also be very

useful. Even if it is imperfect and unenforceable, such planning could help the global network to evolve toward an optimal structure because in many instances, for example, the recommendations of the Consultative Committees, administrations have a stake in taking into account the information and recommendations they receive from ITU. Long-term planning would also benefit the regulatory Administrative Conferences and Consultative Committees by anticipating problems and permitting modifications or studies in good time rather than when it is already almost too late. The stages of this planning process could be the following:

(a) Collection and periodic updating of requirements as this is done, for example, in Intelsat.

(b) Gathering of information concerning national or multinational projects.

(c) Studies, conducted by the Secretariat and subsequently approved by groups or meetings still to be defined, attempting to establish clearly various possible solutions, their economic consequences and the difficulties or obstacles likely to be encountered, and possibly making recommendations to resolve these difficulties (through planning conferences, changes in regulations, studies to be undertaken by the Consultative Committees). The planning process would certainly require the creation within the ITU Secretariat of a new department comprising economic experts who would rely on the secretariats of the Consultative Committees in all technical matters. This department would also be able to assist governments wishing to establish their own planning mechanisms in the field of international telecommunications. ITU's technical assistance operations might well be attached to this department, since the essential aim of this technical assistance is to plan for future telecommunications systems in the developing countries.

Structure of ITU

The structure of ITU should be adapted to its various functions. The future structure must also take into account the present structure, since in practice only a slow evolution seems possible.

The Secretariat. We would suggest that the Secretary-General should be placed under the control of and be responsible to the Administrative Council but should also direct the Secretariat as a whole. The Secretariat would be divided into three large departments, each headed by an Assistant Secretary-General elected by the most appropriate assembly.

The administrative and legal department would be specifically charged with the responsibility for organizing Plenipotentiary and Administrative Conferences (except planning conferences), for the final formulation of regulations and for the administrative tasks (notification, coordination) that now fall upon the IFRB, but would not have to express final opinions, either favorable or unfavorable, on frequency assignments. The administrative and legal department would receive assistance from the technical department whenever necessary during the coordination procedures and could obtain reports or estimates on the dangers of interference; in return, the administrative and legal department would assist the other departments whenever necessary. The administrative and legal department might be formed from the present Secretariat (rearranged and probably excluding the present technical assistance service) and part of the secretariat of the IFRB.

The technical department would combine the CCIR and CCITT secretariats, although initially two distinct sections, one for radio and the other for telephone/telegraph, could be maintained. They would merge only after a more or less extended period. In order not to overburden the meetings of the Consultative Committees, and to facilitiate their ultimate merger, their numerous subcommittees would work separately and only submit their draft texts to the assemblies for final administrative approval. The technical department would also provide technical assistance to the other two departments of the Secretariat and to national telecommunications administrations as described above. The staffs of the present secretariats would expand somewhat as would the participation of representatives of the developing countries. The technical department would have at its disposal the computer center which it would manage for the Secretariat as a whole. If an Assistant Secretary-General were to replace the two present directors of the respective Consultative Committees before the committees had merged, he would be elected by a joint meeting of the assemblies.

The department of planning and economic studies would be newly created in its entirety. It would have to organize and prepare planning conferences and publish their proceedings. Like the Consultative Committees, this department could divide the work of planning among a certain number of international working groups or committees, each with a particular sphere of competence. One of these working groups could be the satellite communication planning group proposed by the Twentieth Century Fund.[2]

The Arbitral Tribunal. The Plenipotentiary Conference could create, preferably at its level, an International Arbitral Tribunal or, to use the Twentieth Century Fund term, a "Frequency Mediation Panel."[3] The tribunal would replace the IFRB in giving final opinions on frequency assignments. The tribunal could also arbitrate serious disputes between administrations and identify violations of the regulations.

In order to keep changes in the present structure to a minimum, we suggest that, at least initially, the tribunal might be composed of five members elected under the same conditions as the present members of the IFRB and with an analogous representation of the different regions. The tribunal should be completely independent of the ITU Secretariat, although the Secretariat would prepare records for examination by the tribunal and would furnish the tribunal with all the elements necessary for its activity. All administrations affected by a decision would be able to communicate their views beforehand in writing or request to be heard by the tribunal. The tribunal could also require the appearance of any telecommunications administration whose views it desired to obtain. Under these conditions, the present role and powers of the IFRB might increase appreciably. But an appeals procedure should also be available for parties

[2] *The Future of Satellite Communications: Resource Management and the Needs of Nations*, Second Report of the Twentieth Century Fund Task Force on International Satellite Communications, The Twentieth Century Fund, New York, 1970, p. 25.
[3] *Ibid.*, p. 26.

contesting the tribunal's judgments. If the Arbitral Tribunal is to retain the last word, the Secretariat might be responsible for formulating a preliminary judgment.

Conclusion

The ITU structure proposed here is extremely simplified and idealized; the reality necessarily will be much more complex. But the general lines that seem desirable for the evolution of ITU can be summarized as follows:

With regard to the Secretariat:

- Unification, enabling it to deal synthetically and simultaneously, rather than separately, with the various aspects of telecommunications;
- Activity directed more towards the future, enabling the Secretariat to anticipate and "manage" the development of the global telecommunications network, rather than merely to follow it;
- A more important role in the preparation, elaboration and presentation of data and of decisions, not to deprive national telecommunications administrations of final choice but to lighten the burden that they now bear;
- Increased and more systematic assistance to countries that request it;

With regard to the IFRB:

- Increased powers along lines appropriate to a genuine Arbitral Tribunal;
- Similarly increased powers to defend the interests of the developing countries, particularly against the consequences of the "first come, first served" principle, now in force.